Life in the UK Test
Study Guide

The essential study guide for the British citizenship test

Published by Red Squirrel Publishing

Red Squirrel Publishing

Suite 235, 77 Beak Street,

London W1F 9DB, United Kingdom

www.redsquirrelbooks.com

First edition published in 2006

Sixth Edition – Fourth Impression

Study Guide: ISBN 978-1-907389-06-1

Study Guide + CD ROM: ISBN 978-1-907389-07-8

Edited by Henry Dillon & George Sandison

Proofreading by Kelly Jones

Designed and typeset by Cox Design Limited, Witney, Oxon

Printed and bound in Aberwystwyth by Cambrian

Table of Contents

Introduction

Choosing to make the United Kingdom your permanent home is an exciting decision made by over 200,000 people every year. However, the decision to become a British citizen or permanent resident is only the start of what can be a long and challenging journey. The application process is complex, time-consuming and expensive.

An important part of the process is the Life in the UK Test. The test requires you to learn about life in this country based on information provided by the Home Office. This book is designed to make this stage in the process a whole lot easier.

Home Office statistics show that over one in four people fail the test. At £50 for every test taken, this is an expensive mistake, and an unnecessary one. By using this book to learn the required material, you can walk into your test confident that you will be one of the people who pass the test on their first attempt, and you will be one important step closer to making Britain your home.

Get in touch

We are always delighted when we hear from our readers. If you have any comments or questions about your studies and test, the book or website, or would like to share a particular experience, please get in touch with us.

With your help we can improve our products to help thousands more people.

To send us feedback please visit:
www.lifeintheuk.net/feedback

Find us on Facebook
www.facebook.com/lifeintheuk

Follow us on Twitter
@lifeintheuk

WHAT'S NEW IN 2012?

We've made some changes to this edition of the study guide, including adding:

- our new Watch & Learn videos that help you understand some of the more complicated topics
- details of the new test booking process and ESOL criteria introduced by the UKBA
- extra notes based on valuable reader feedback

How to Watch and Learn

If you have a smartphone, the quickest way to access the Watch & Learn videos is by scanning the QR codes you will find in the text. The QR codes look like square barcodes; you can see one on page 8 of this Introduction.

You will need a barcode reader app to scan the QR codes; you can download one for free from the App Store or Android Marketplace.

If you don't have a smartphone then don't worry - you can still watch the content on your computer by using the website address below the QR codes.

Out-of-date material

The official study materials in this edition have not changed since they were updated 2007. Therefore, you may notice that some of the facts in this book are out of date.

Despite this material being out of date, the Home Office has advised all candidates that they will only be tested on the published study materials and not on the latest laws or facts.

Whilst some of the information that follows may be out of date, it is safer to learn this rather than risk failing your test.

We have highlighted the main areas where material is out of date and given a summary of how things have changed.

A complete list of this out-of-date material can be found at www.lifeintheuk.net/out-of-date. You can also find updated contact details for all organisations listed in the study material at www.lifeintheuk.net/contact_details.

How to use this study guide

This study guide has many parts and features, but the parts of the book that you must focus on for your test are the official study materials (see **chapters 2–6**). These study materials have been reproduced in full from the Home Office publication, *Life in the United Kingdom: A Journey to Citizenship*. You must make sure you read and understand these parts as the questions that you will be asked when you sit your test are all based on these chapters only.

The study materials are divided into five easy-to-learn chapters:

• A Changing Society

• UK Today: A Profile

• How the United Kingdom is Governed

• Everyday Needs

• Employment

Chapter 1 includes information on the application process as well as advice from people who passed the test and answers to some of their most common questions.

The other parts of this book support the study materials by making them easier to understand and learn. There are also practice tests that will help you prepare for your test by checking your knowledge.

Extra revision notes

This guide contains extra revision notes that summarise the study materials from all five chapters. Included in this is an extensive glossary of words that you need to know. These are words or phrases that you will need to understand for your test, or are terms that you may need to know to give you background to the official study materials. Each word or phrase is explained fully, in easy-to-understand language. As you work your way through the materials, you can use the **Words to know** section to check any terms or expressions that are not familiar.

Practice questions

Once you've finished revising the study materials, try answering the practice questions. This will help you test your knowledge and identify any areas which you need to study further.

Further practice tests, along with news and up-to-date information about the material in this guide can also be found online at www.lifeintheuk.net.

After your test

In the final part of this guide, you'll find useful information that will help you with your citizenship ceremony. There is also information to help you complete your application for citizenship and apply for a British passport.

Register your book

When you are ready to start taking practice tests you can use your Study Guide to claim a free subscription to the online tests at www.lifeintheuk.net/test.

Once you have created your account follow the instructions to get a free 24-hour subscription. You can claim this free subscription as many times as you like.

Get the BritTest app on your iPhone

Take practice tests wherever you go with hundreds of questions and randomised practice tests in your hand.

The essential revision aid for anyone on the move. Available from **www.lifeintheuk.net/app** and the App Store.

You can scan this QR code with your iPhone and go straight to the App Store. If you can't scan it, you can download a free barcode reader app.

CHAPTER 1
About the Test

→ THE LIFE IN THE UK TEST is designed to test your knowledge of British life and ability to use English.

The Life in the UK Test was first introduced in November 2005 as a requirement for anyone applying for British citizenship. From 2 April 2007 this requirement was extended to include people seeking to permanently settle in the UK.

- Applicants are given 45 minutes to complete the test.
- The test is made up of 24 multiple-choice questions.
- Questions are chosen at random by computer.
- The pass mark is 75% (18 questions correct out of 24).
- Each attempt to pass the test costs £50.
- The test is conducted at around 60 Life in the UK Test centres across the UK.
- Applicants sit the test using a computer, which is provided by the test centre.
- Just under 71% of applicants pass the test (as at November 2009).

Who needs to take the test?

In order to be granted settlement and/or naturalisation as a British citizen you need to demonstrate 'knowledge of language and life in the UK'. By passing the Life in the UK Test you meet this requirement.

INDEFINITE LEAVE TO REMAIN (ILR)

If you have lived in the UK legally for a certain length of time – normally between two and five years, depending on your visa – categories that allow an application for ILR in the UK include:

- Ancestry or legal residence under a work permit or Tier of the points-based system – after five years.
- Highly Skilled Migrant Programme (HSMP) – after five years.
- Married to/Partner of a British citizen, or a person settled in the UK – after two years.
- Long residency – after ten years' legal residency, or 14 years as a combination of illegal and legal residency.

If your application for ILR is successful then you will be free from immigration time restrictions and allowed to live and work in the country lawfully with no time limits. Once you get ILR you should not spend periods longer than two years outside of the UK. Settled residents should consider the UK their home, so spending small periods of time here may lead to ILR being revoked.

Once your application for ILR has been approved you are able to apply for public benefits, subject to eligibility.

For applicants seeking to remain as the spouse or partner of a British citizen, or someone settled in the UK, you must intend to continue the marriage and be able to show:

- you were given permission to enter/remain in the country on a marriage/partner visa
- that you have completed the residency requirement
- evidence of your cohabitation and your ability to support yourself and your family.

NATURALISATION

You are eligible to apply for British citizenship 12 months after you are granted ILR, or are otherwise freed from immigration time restrictions. You must have also completed the residency period, which is normally five years (or three years as the spouse or partner of a British citizen).

If you have not taken the Life in the UK Test yet, and are not exempt as below, you will need to take it before you can apply.

ESOL and alternatives to the test

If your English skills are below ESOL Entry 3 level (or Intermediate 1 level in Scotland) you must take the ESOL course in English with citizenship. If you are having difficulty reading the English in this book then you should consider the combined English language (ESOL) and citizenship classes instead of taking the Life in the UK Test.

The courses are extremely popular and often have waiting lists. To find out where courses are available in your area check www.direct.gov.uk or contact the Life in the UK Test Helpline on 0800 015 4245.

If you take the ESOL course you must be sure that:

- Your course is run at an accredited college and your qualification is from an approved awarding body

- The course includes material from *Citizenship Materials for ESOL Learners* (ISBN: 1844785424)

- You make 'relevant progress' of at least one level.

For more information see the *ESOL course in English with Citizenship* page of the UK Border Office website, www.ukba.homeoffice.gov.uk.

Only combined ESOL for citizenship courses can be used instead of taking the Life in the UK Test. Make sure that the course you choose is the correct one.

Who is exempt from taking the test?

CITIZENSHIP

You are only exempt from taking the test when applying for citizenship if:

• you are under 18 years of age or over 65 years of age, or

• you have a significant physical or mental health condition. This condition must permanently prevent you from studying for or taking the test, or an ESOL qualification.

If you have a disability that exempts you from taking the test then you will need to obtain evidence of this from a qualified medical practitioner. If your condition responds to treatment you will be expected to prepare yourself for the test.

If you have a visual or hearing impairment this will not exempt you from the test. Most test centres are well equipped to assist people with such disabilities. Check with your local test centre to see if they can accommodate you.

ILR

There are more exemptions for people who are applying for permanent residence. As well as those above, the following are exempt:

• foreign and Commonwealth citizens on discharge from HM Forces (including Ghurkhas), and their spouses or partners

• victims of domestic violence

• bereaved spouses, unmarried partners or civil partners of someone who was settled in the UK

• parents, grandparents and other dependent relatives living in exceptionally compassionate circumstances, who are joining a person already present and settled in the UK

• retired persons of independent means

• EU nationals, or non-European family members of EU nationals under the Free Movement of Persons provisions

- refugees with five years residence

- people on discretionary leave with six years residence

- people with exceptional leave to remain and four years residence

- someone who has spent five years in the UK with humanitarian protection

- dependent children of businessmen, self-employed people, investors, writers, composers or artists. This includes children over 18, as long as they are dependent

- Turkish business people under the ECAA agreement

- spouses, civil partners, unmarried or same sex partners of British citizens or persons settled in the UK, who are permanent members of HM Diplomatic Service; staff members of the British Council on a tour of duty abroad; and staff members of the Department for International Development.

These exemptions only apply to settlement applications. If you apply for British citizenship later on, you will need to take the test, unless exempt as above.

How to pass your test

STEP 1: BOOK YOUR TEST

You must now book for the test online through the UKBA website. You will need valid photo ID, a debit or credit card and an email address to book. You must pay the test fee when you book.

You will be directed to the test centres closest to you when you book. You can also call the Life in the UK Test Helpline on 0800 015 4245 for more information.

You should expect to wait a few weeks for your test appointment. This is normal and provides you with a date to focus your study towards. Tests are carried out at around 60 test centres through-out the UK.

Information released by Ufi, the company which runs the test centres, shows that the average waiting time for a test is about 15 days. Make sure you plan ahead and book your test for a day that suits you.

STEP 2: STUDY THE MATERIALS

Once you have a test appointment, you can study with that date in mind as a goal.

All the questions that can be asked in the Life in the UK Test are based on the official study materials provided by the Home Office. The relevant material has been fully reproduced in this guide.

Before you start studying, note that your official test will only ask questions based on chapters 2, 3, 4, 5 and 6 of the Home Office publication. The questions in this book are also drawn only from those chapters.

Some of the facts that you need to learn for your test relate to laws and regulations determined and administered by the government. The study materials in this book were published by the Home Office in February 2007. Since that time, some laws and regulations have changed, meaning that some facts in this book are out of date.

The Home Office advises that you will only be tested on the published study materials and not on the latest laws or regulations.

While these changes to laws and regulations will not be reflected in your test, some of them affect important topics that you may need to know about. We have highlighted the major changes in the text. A detailed list of all the changes made since publication can be found on our website by visiting www.lifeintheuk. net/out-of-date.

STEP 3: TAKE PRACTICE TESTS

Once you've finished thoroughly reviewing the study materials you should check if you are ready to take the official test by completing several practice tests from this book. It is important to make sure that you fully understand the chapters and haven't just memorised the information as written.

Each of the practice tests is different and contains 24 questions. Each test contains questions covering all parts of the study materials. These questions will not necessarily be phrased in the same way as the study materials.

If you do not pass the practice tests consistently, or do not feel confident enough to sit your official test, then you should continue your study. If you do not have sufficient time left before your official test to do more study, then you may be able to reschedule your test appointment. You can cancel your test without charge up to seven days before your test. If you cancel within seven days your test fee will not be refunded. You will have to book and pay again. You can change your test appointment using your online account on the UKBA website.

Some of the questions asked in your test may be specific to the part of Britain where you are taking your test. If you are taking the test in Scotland, Wales or Northern Ireland then you should make sure you understand the information in the study materials that is specific to where you live.

Once you've finished with the questions in this book, additional questions can be found in our separate publication *Life in the UK Test: Practice Questions* or the *BritTest* app in the App Store. You can also go online and access further tests with our free subscription offer; visit www.lifeintheuk.net to redeem this offer.

> The practice questions in this book have been designed to help you check you have acquired the knowledge you need to pass the test. Although they are not the same questions that you will receive in your official test, they are in the same format, use the same approach and test you on the same official material. **The practice tests are not a substitute for reading and understanding chapters 2–6**.
>
> Although the official questions that are used in the test are kept secret, thousands of our readers have told us that the practice questions in this book were very similar to the actual questions that they received in their test.

STEP 4: TAKE AND PASS YOUR TEST

Firstly, it is important to make sure that you have a good night's sleep before the test and that you have eaten beforehand as well. It may surprise you, but being tired or hungry can severely affect your concentration and make the test harder for you.

Make sure you take proof of your address, such as a gas/water bill, bank statement or letter from the Home Office. You must also take the photographic ID you used when you booked your test with you. This ID must be valid and not expired. The following types are acceptable forms of photographic ID:

- a passport from your country of origin – this document may be out of date

- a UK photocard driving licence, full or provisional

- one of the following Home Office travel documents: a Convention Travel Document (CTD), a Certificate of Identity Document (CID) or a Stateless Persons' Document (SPD) – this document must be in date

- an Immigration Status Document, endorsed with a UK Residence Permit and bearing a photo of the holder – this document may be out of date, or

- a Home Office Identity Card.

If you have had previous contact with the Home Office (for example, when applying for an extension of stay) then you will have been issued with a Home Office reference number. You should take this number with you when you take your test, and provide it to the test supervisor when asked.

When you arrive at the test centre you will need to register your details and sign an attendee list to confirm your attendance.

You will take the test using a computer provided at the test centre. You will be allowed to run through a few practice questions so that you are familiar with the test software. Some applicants worry that they do not know the answers for the practice questions, however the results of the practice questions do not affect your end result.

The whole process leading up to the test itself may take some time as there may be many candidates to register.

Make sure you listen carefully when the test supervisor explains how to use the test software. It is important that you know how to use it. If you are unsure then ask the test supervisor for help. As each applicant's test is begun individually by the test supervisor, your test will not begin until you say that you are ready.

Once your test begins you will have 45 minutes to complete it. In 2007, Ufi announced that one in three candidates completed the test within 15 minutes and 80% of candidates completed the test within 30 minutes. You will be able to review and change the answers to your questions at any stage during the test.

If you pass then you will be given a Pass Notification Letter, which you should sign before you leave the test centre. This is an important document and must be attached to your settlement or citizenship application.

You will not be able to get a replacement Pass Notification Letter if you lose it. Make sure you keep it in a safe place.

If you don't pass then you can take the test again, however you will need to book and pay for another appointment. You must wait at least seven days before retaking your test. You should not make an application for naturalisation as a British citizen or for indefinite leave to remain if you fail. You may need to apply for further leave to remain if your existing leave to remain has expired, or is close to expiring.

Advice from our readers

Our readers often contact us to share their advice and experiences of taking the test. This section is a summary of the most common and insightful comments that we have received.

> The test was supposed to start at 1pm but in reality it started almost one hour later. When they make the appointments they should inform us that the test is 45 minutes but the whole process might take longer

While the test itself lasts 45 minutes, the whole process of the test can last much longer. You need to arrive well before your scheduled start time, and allow time for registration and the various other administrative procedures that the test supervisor needs to carry out before and after the test. Some candidates have reported the process taking up to two and a half hours. You should bear this in mind if you are driving to the test and need to park, or have other commitments on the day.

> The whole process of checking ID and logging on took an hour!

The registration process at the test centre can take a long time. Depending on the size of the test centre and the number of people booked for your particular test registering them all, perhaps one at a time, can be lengthy. The test supervisor needs to check that all candidates taking the test are who they say are. This is very important for the integrity of the test.

> I thought I'd get a breakdown of my results that day

At the end of the test, you will only be told whether you passed or failed. You will not be told your score or how many answers you got wrong. If you failed, you will only be told which chapters you need to spend more time studying again.

> The official questions were worded differently to the online test questions and the book

It is highly likely that you will not have seen the exact questions that are in the test before. The practice tests are intended to help you prepare and get used to the style of questions you will get in your real test. It is very important that you read the question carefully and are sure you understand it before you answer.

> One question about taxes confused me a bit; but after a thorough analysis of the question I remembered reading about it in your book and found the right answer

Whenever you encounter difficult questions, remember that if you have read all the chapters in the book you will have come across the answer before. You should take your time and make sure you fully understand the question, thinking about each alternative answer, before submitting what you think is the correct answer.

> I have taken the test twice but failed both times. It would be helpful if they had a translation of the test and the book in my language

The test serves two purposes: It tests your understanding of the study materials and it tests that you can read and understand English. If you cannot read English well then you are unlikely to pass the test. If you find that your command of English is not good enough to pass the test you have two options. You can either improve your English through study and practice or you can take a special citizenship-based ESOL course.

More information about ESOL courses can be found at www.direct.gov.uk, including contact numbers for call centres which provide advice in other languages.

> There was variation from the questions I had practised. I was, however, able to cope with this easily as the practice tests had given me a broader knowledge and confidence to answer any new questions with ease

To perform at your best on the day of the test it will help if you feel calm and confident. This is part of what doing practice tests offers you through reinforcing your understanding of the material. Once you can consistently pass the practice tests, you will know that you are very familiar with what you have been learning. You can then walk into your test with the knowledge that you are fully prepared and ready to answer whatever questions you are asked.

> I failed because I relied on the practice tests and did not study the chapters in any detail

Just taking practice tests is not sufficient preparation. Questions in your test can be taken from every part of chapters 2, 3, 4, 5 and

6 of the book. It is very unlikely that you will understand all of the material you may be tested on just by taking the practice tests. In addition to taking practice tests, you should read the study materials thoroughly.

> I took the test in Wales and didn't expect to have so many 'Wales'-based questions

Tests are different depending on the region where they are being held. Tests taken in Wales, Northern Ireland and Scotland will include questions specific to those nations. The number of questions in your individual test that will relate to your region can't be predicted, but you should expect several such questions.

> I did not feel comfortable asking the test centre staff for help

The test supervisors are there to help you. If you are unsure of anything then you must ask. They will assist you if you have any problems with your computer or if you are uncomfortable in any way, but they will not help you with the answers!

> The computer I was using froze during my test. I found it very disturbing and was unable to concentrate as a result

Unfortunately we have had reports of computers at test centres being faulty. These include faults with the equipment you are given, such as a malfunctioning screen or a mouse that doesn't work properly. We have also received reports of other windows popping up in front of the test questions. This may be a result of the computer being infected with a virus or other malicious software and should not happen.

If you have any sort of a problem with your computer, you should inform the test supervisor immediately. If they can't correct the problem to your satisfaction you should ask to be moved to another computer. You must be given the opportunity to take your test on properly functioning equipment.

> I didn't realise 30 of us would take the test at the same time

You will not be taking the test alone. You will be taking the test with a number of other people who have booked the same time at your test centre. This can be quite a large number, depending on the size of the test centre. The number of people taking the test at one time does not affect your test in any way. You will be given your own computer and your own space. There will be enough room for everyone there to take the test, all at the same time.

> I was surprised that I wasn't given the same questions as the other candidates sitting the test at the same time as me

Every candidate gets their own unique set of questions in the test. The test centres have access to a database containing hundreds of questions and each candidate's questions are selected at random by computer. This minimises the risk of candidates cheating by looking at each other's computer monitors.

> My daughter and husband were not allowed to wait for me in the building. We should have been told about this before the test

Every test centre is different. Some may have a waiting area for friends or family, whilst others may not. If you intend to be accompanied by friends or family members, we suggest you call the test centre in advance to see if there is somewhere they can wait for you there.

I am not sure if my study text is up to date with the current test

It is absolutely vital that you study from a current book. The Home Office updates the official study material from time to time. It is also possible that bookshops may sell you an older version of the book even though we do everything we can to make sure they only have the latest edition in stock. The best way to be sure you have the latest edition of the book is to check our website, www.lifeintheuk.net. If you have been sold an out-of-date edition of the book, you should try to return it to the shop where you bought it.

I was told that this study guide was the wrong one

Staff at some test centres may tell you that you have been using the wrong book to study – this is not true. Although the government's own study guide is the official version, there are many other independent guides that offer exactly the same material but also provide additional advice that the official guide does not. For instance, we endeavour to give you the information you need to pass your test and the up-to-date information where the official guide is now out of date. The only thing you need to check is that the book you are using is up to date and has been published by a reputable publisher.

Your application – common problems

A small percentage of citizenship applications are refused. In 2009 over 10,000 applications, making up 5% of the total, were with-drawn; the top five reasons for these refusals were as follows:

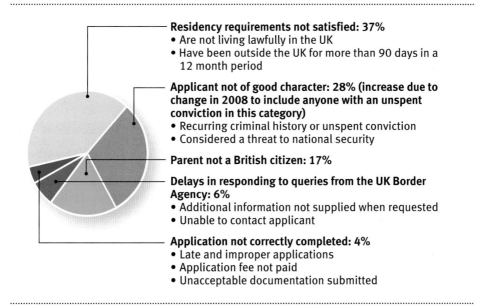

Residency requirements not satisfied: 37%
- Are not living lawfully in the UK
- Have been outside the UK for more than 90 days in a 12 month period

Applicant not of good character: 28% (increase due to change in 2008 to include anyone with an unspent conviction in this category)
- Recurring criminal history or unspent conviction
- Considered a threat to national security

Parent not a British citizen: 17%

Delays in responding to queries from the UK Border Agency: 6%
- Additional information not supplied when requested
- Unable to contact applicant

Application not correctly completed: 4%
- Late and improper applications
- Application fee not paid
- Unacceptable documentation submitted

You should not send your application more than 28 days before you become eligible to apply. If you do the UK Border Agency may refuse your application on grounds of the residency requirements not being satisfied and they will not refund any fees paid. However, you must ensure you make your application before your current permission to stay in the UK expires.

You should note that in 2008 the definition of good character was changed; now, any applications made will be refused if the applicant has been convicted of a criminal offence and the conviction has not yet been spent.

A very small percentage were also refused because the applicant did not attend their citizenship ceremony in time – make sure this isn't you!

NEW EVIDENCE IN APPEALS

The UKBA no longer accept any late evidence submitted after an application has been made in appeals.

This means if your application is refused you cannot appeal on the grounds that you forgot to, or could not, send in any information. Exceptions and mitigating circumstances will not be considered. You will also not get a refund of your application fee.

If you want to check that your application is complete you can use the Settlement and Nationality Checking Services offered by most local authorities. These services have two main advantages:

1. Your application, along with all supporting documentation, will be checked and completed correctly before being sent ensuring it is processed promptly.

2. Certified copies are taken of valuable supporting documents – such as passports – allowing you to keep the originals.

A directory of councils offering this service can be found on our website, www.lifeintheuk.net/ncs. There is a fee payable for this service – the amount depends on your local council. This service is very popular, so make sure you contact them before you want to send your application to ensure you get an appointment.

Absences during the residency period

You should already know that in order to get ILR or British Citizenship there are limits on the amount of time you can spend outside the UK. What you may not realise is that the restrictions are more strict for ILR than citizenship.

INDEFINITE LEAVE TO REMAIN (ILR)

If you are applying for ILR and you have absences totalling more than 180 days during your residence period you may have your application refused. You residence will also be considered broken if you are away from the UK for more than 90 days in one go.

If you are applying as the spouse or partner of a British citizen or permanent resident then the Immigration Rules do not provide clear guidance. In these cases the UKBA advise that your application 'will be judged on its merits, taking into account your reasons for travel, the length of your absences, and whether you and your partner travelled and lived together while you were outside the UK.' We advise against long absences, where possible.

The new categories under Tier 1 for entrepreneurs and investors have less strict residence requirements. People applying for ILR in these categories are allowed 180 days absence from the UK in any 12 months.

This extra flexibility has been given because investors and entrepreneurs are expected to need to travel outside of the UK to fulfil business and investment obligations.

CITIZENSHIP

For citizenship applications, absences from the UK should be limited to 90 days for each year of your qualifying period, and 90 days in the 12 months before your application.

Applications made after five year's residence allow for 450 days absence, with 90 in the last year.

The UKBA say they 'normally disregard' absences of up to 300 days. Long absences may need to be explained, but it helps if you have settled your home, family and a large part of your estate in the UK.

Consideration may be given for absences over the limits in certain circumstances – for instance, if journeys outside the UK were made for compassionate reasons, or were to do with your employment.

In the 12 months before your application the UKBA 'normally disregard' absences of up to 100 days. Longer absences may need to be explained as above.

Test Preparation Checklist

There are a lot of things that you need to remember to do for the Life in the UK Test. Avoid problems and get organised by completing this checklist.

◯ **Test appointment booked**

- Book your test through the UKBA website

- Test Date

- Time

- Test Centre Address

- Phone

◯ **Finished reading study materials (see chapters 2–6)**

◯ **Completed all practice tests in study guide**

◯ **Completed free online practice tests at www.lifeintheuk.net**

◯ **Checked latest tips and advice at www.lifeintheuk.net**

◯ **Photographic ID and proof of address arranged**

◯ **Test centre location and travel route confirmed**

CHAPTER 2
A Changing Society

→ IN THIS CHAPTER you will learn about how British society has changed in recent times. The chapter mainly focuses on how different groups have contributed to society since the end of the Second World War. Think about why migrants wanted to come to Britain, but also consider why Britain wanted and needed new immigrants. Concentrate on how women have gained more rights and responsibilities, particularly in politics, education and the workplace. Also think about differences that have developed in how women contribute in their more traditional family roles, especially in terms of childcare. When reading the section on children and young people consider how families have changed in Britain. Also focus on the challenges that face children and young people today as they progress through the education system and become young adults.

IN THIS CHAPTER THERE IS INFORMATION ABOUT:

Migration to Britain
- The long history of immigration to the United Kingdom
- Different reasons why people migrated to the UK
- Basic changes in immigration patterns over the last 30 years

The changing role of women
- Changes to family structures and women's rights since the 19th century
- Women's campaigns for rights, including the right to vote, in the late 19th and early 20th centuries
- Discrimination against women in the workplace and in education
- Changing attitudes to women working, and responsibilities of men and women in the home

Children, family and young people
- The identity, interests, tastes and lifestyle patterns of children and young people
- Education and work
- Health hazards: cigarettes, alcohol and illegal drugs
- Young people's political and social attitudes

Migration to Britain

Many people living in Britain today have their origins in other countries. They can trace their roots to regions throughout the world such as Europe, the Middle East, Africa, Asia and the Caribbean. In the distant past, invaders came to Britain, seized land and stayed. More recently, people come to Britain to find safety, jobs and a better life.

Britain is proud of its tradition of offering safety to people who are escaping persecution and hardship. For example, in the 16th and 18th centuries, Huguenots (French Protestants) came to Britain to escape religious persecution in France. In the mid-1840s there was a terrible famine in Ireland and many Irish people migrated to Britain. Many Irish men became labourers and helped to build canals and railways across Britain.

> **"**
> The UK encouraged immigration in the 1950s for economic reasons and many industries advertised for workers from overseas.
> **"**

From 1880 to 1910, a large number of Jewish people came to Britain to escape racist attacks (called 'pogroms') in what was then called the Russian Empire and from the countries now called Poland, Ukraine and Belarus.

MIGRATION SINCE 1945

After the Second World War (1939–45), there was a huge task of rebuilding Britain. There were not enough people to do the work, so the British Government encouraged workers from Ireland and other parts of Europe to come to the UK to help with the reconstruction. In 1948, people from the West Indies were also invited to come and work.

During the 1950s, there was still a shortage of labour in the UK. The UK encouraged immigration in the 1950s for economic reasons and many industries advertised for workers from overseas. For example, centres were set up in the West Indies to recruit people to drive buses. Textile and engineering firms from the north of England and the Midlands sent agents to India and Pakistan to find workers. For about 25 years, people from the West Indies, India, Pakistan, and later Bangladesh, travelled to work and settle in Britain.

The number of people migrating from these areas fell in the late 1960s and early 70s because the government passed new laws to restrict immigration to Britain, although immigrants from 'old'

Commonwealth countries such as Australia, New Zealand and Canada did not have to face such strict controls.

During this time, however, the UK was able to help a large number of refugees. In 1972 the UK accepted thousands of people of Indian origin who had been forced to leave Uganda. Another programme to help people from Vietnam was introduced in the late 1970s. Since 1979, more than 25,000 refugees from South East Asia have been allowed to settle in the UK.

In the 1980s the largest immigrant groups came from the United States, Australia, South Africa and New Zealand. In the early 1990s, groups of people from the former Soviet Union came to Britain looking for a new and safer way of life. Since 1994 there has been a global rise in mass migration for both political and economic reasons.

Check that you understand: ✔

- some of the historical reasons for immigration to the UK

- some of the reasons for immigration to the UK since 1945, and

- the main immigrant groups coming to the UK since 1945, the countries they came from and the kind of work they did.

Watch & Learn:

www.lifeintheuk.net/2012ec2

Scan to watch a video that explains all the immigrant groups that came to the UK

The changing role of women

In 19th-century Britain, families were usually large and in many poorer homes men, women and children all contributed towards the family income. Although they made an important economic contribution, women in Britain had fewer rights than men. Until 1857, a married woman had no right to divorce her husband. Until 1882, when a woman got married, her earnings, property and money automatically belonged to her husband.

In the late 19th and early 20th centuries, an increasing number of women campaigned and demonstrated for greater rights and, in particular, the right to vote. They became known as 'Suffragettes'. These protests decreased during the First World War because women joined in the war effort and therefore did a much greater variety of work than they had before. When the First World War ended in 1918, women over the age of 30 were finally given the right to vote and to stand for election to parliament. It was not until 1928 that women won the right to vote at 21, at the same age as men.

> **66**
> These days girls leave school, on average, with better qualifications than boys and there are now more women than men at university.
> **99**

Despite these improvements, women still faced discrimination in the workplace. For example, it was quite common for employers to ask women to leave their jobs when they got married. Many jobs were closed to women and it was difficult for women to enter universities. During the 1960s and 1970s there was increasing pressure from women for equal rights. Parliament passed new laws giving women the right to equal pay and prohibiting employers from discriminating against women because of their sex (see also **Chapter 6**).

WOMEN IN BRITAIN TODAY

Women in Britain today make up 51% of the population and 45% of the workforce. These days girls leave school, on average, with better qualifications than boys and there are now more women than men at university.

UK population by gender

Male 49% Female 51%

UK workforce

Male 55% Female 45%

The 2011 Census results are due in 2012, and may not agree with this. However, for the purposes of your test you must learn the figures as based on the 2001 Census.

Employment opportunities for women are now much greater than they were in the past. Although women continue to be employed in traditional female areas such as healthcare, teaching, secretarial and retail work, there is strong evidence that attitudes are changing, and women are now active in a much wider range of work than before. Research shows that very few people today believe that women in Britain should stay at home and not go out to work. Today, almost three-quarters of women with school-age children are in paid work.

In most households, women continue to have the main responsibility for childcare and housework. There is evidence that there is now greater equality in homes and that more men are taking some responsibility for raising the family and doing housework. Despite this progress, many people believe that more needs to be done to achieve greater equality for women. There are still examples of discrimination against women, particularly in the workplace, despite the laws that exist to prevent it. Women still do not always have the same access to promotion and better-paid jobs. The average hourly pay rate for women is 20% less than for men, and after leaving university most women still earn less than men.

66
The average hourly pay rate for women is 20% less than for men, and after leaving university most women still earn less than men.
99

Check that you understand:

- when women aged over 30 were first given the right to vote
- when women were given equal voting rights with men, and
- some of the important developments to create equal rights in the workplace.

Children, family and young people

In the UK, there are almost 15 million children and young people up to the age of 19. This is almost one-quarter of the UK population.

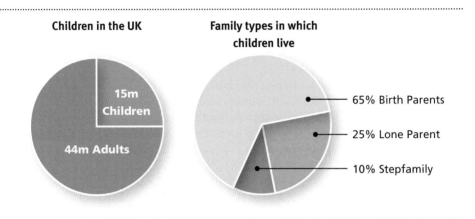

Children in the UK

15m Children

44m Adults

Family types in which children live

65% Birth Parents

25% Lone Parent

10% Stepfamily

> **"** Most children in Britain receive weekly pocket money from their parents and many get extra money for doing jobs around the house. **"**

Over the last 20 years, family patterns in Britain have been transformed because of the changing attitudes towards divorce and separation. Today, 65% of children live with both birth parents, almost 25% live in lone-parent families and 10% live within a stepfamily. Most children in Britain receive weekly pocket money from their parents and many get extra money for doing jobs around the house.

Children in the UK do not play outside the home as much as they did in the past. Part of the reason for this is increased home entertainment such as television, videos and computers. There is also increased concern for children's safety and there are many stories in newspapers about child molestation by strangers, but there is no evidence that this kind of danger is increasing.

Young people have different identities, interests and fashions to older people. Many young people move away from their family home when they become adults but this varies from one community to another.

EDUCATION

The law states that children between the ages of 5 and 16 must attend school. The tests that pupils take are very important, and in England and Scotland children take national tests in English, mathematics and science when they are 7, 11 and 14 years old. (In Wales, teachers assess children's progress when they are 7 and 11 and they take a national test at the age of 14.) The tests give important information about children's progress and achievement, the subjects they are doing well in and the areas where they need extra help.

Most young people take the General Certificate of Secondary Education (GCSE), or, in Scotland, Scottish Qualifications Authority (SQA) Standard Grade examinations when they are 16. At 17 and 18, many take vocational qualifications, General Certificates of Education at an Advanced level (AGCEs), AS-level units or Higher/ Advanced Higher Grades in Scotland. Schools and colleges will expect good GCSE or SQA Standard Grade results before allowing a student to enrol on an AGCE or Scottish Higher/Advanced Higher course.

AS-levels are Advanced Subsidiary qualifications gained by completing three AS units. Three AS units are considered as one-half of an AGCE. In the second part of the course, three more AS units can be studied to complete the AGCE qualification.

Many people refer to AGCEs by the old name of A-levels. AGCEs are the traditional route for entry to higher education courses, but many higher education students enter with different kinds of qualifications.

One in three young people now go on to higher education at college or university. Some young people defer their university entrance for a year and take a 'gap year'. This year out of education often includes voluntary work and travel overseas. Some young people work to earn and save money to pay for their university fees and living expenses.

People over 16 years of age may also choose to study at Colleges of Further Education or Adult Education Centres. There is a wide range of academic and vocational courses available as well as courses which develop leisure interests and skills. Contact your local college for details.

Since 2008 there have been many changes in the national curriculums of England, Scotland and Wales. For details on these please see www. lifeintheuk.net. For the purposes of your test you must learn the text as reproduced here. See also p87.

The earliest legal age a child can work is 13, although usually they do not work before 14.

See page 113 for more information.

WORK

It is common for young people to have a part-time job while they are still at school. It is thought there are 2 million children at work at any one time. The most common jobs are newspaper delivery and work in supermarkets and newsagents. Many parents believe that part-time work helps children to become more independent as well as providing them (and sometimes their families) with extra income.

There are laws about the age when children can take up paid work (usually not before 14), the type of work they can do and the number of hours they can work (see www.worksmart.org.uk for more information).

It is very important to note that there are concerns for the safety of children who work illegally or who are not properly supervised, and the employment of children is strictly controlled by law (see **Chapter 6**).

HEALTH HAZARDS

Many parents worry that their children may misuse drugs and addictive substances.

SMOKING

Young people under the age of 18 are not allowed to buy alcohol in Britain, but there is concern about the age some young people start drinking alcohol and the amount of alcohol they drink at one time, known as 'binge drinking'.

Although cigarette smoking has fallen in the adult population, more young people are smoking, and more school-age girls smoke than boys. From 1 October 2007, it is illegal to sell tobacco products to anyone under 18 years old. Smoking is generally not allowed in public buildings and workplaces throughout the UK.

ALCOHOL

Young people under the age of 18 are not allowed to buy alcohol in Britain, but there is concern about the age some young people start drinking alcohol and the amount of alcohol they drink at one time, known as 'binge drinking'. It is illegal to be drunk in public and there are now more penalties to help control this problem, including on-the-spot fines.

ILLEGAL DRUGS

As in most countries, it is illegal to possess drugs such as heroin, cocaine, ecstasy, amphetamines and cannabis. Current statistics show that half of all young adults, and about a third of the population as a whole, have used illegal drugs at one time or another.

There is a strong link between the use of hard drugs (e.g. crack cocaine and heroin) and crime, and also hard drugs and mental illness. The misuse of drugs has a huge social and financial cost for the country. This is a serious issue and British society needs to find an effective way of dealing with the problem.

YOUNG PEOPLE'S POLITICAL AND SOCIAL ATTITUDES

Young people in Britain can vote in elections from the age of 18. In the 2001 general election, however, only 1 in 5 first-time voters used their vote. There has been a great debate over the reasons for this. Some researchers think that one reason is that young people are not interested in the political process.

Although most young people show little interest in party politics, there is strong evidence that many are interested in specific political issues such as the environment and cruelty to animals.

In 2003 a survey of young people in England and Wales showed that they believe the five most important issues in Britain were crime, drugs, war/terrorism, racism and health. The same survey asked young people about their participation in political and community events. They found that 86% of young people had taken part in some form of community event over the past year, and 50% had taken part in fund-raising or collecting money for charity. Similar results have been found in surveys in Scotland and Northern Ireland. Many children first get involved in these activities while at school where they study citizenship as part of the National Curriculum.

In the 2001 general election, only 1 in 5 first-time voters used their vote.

Check that you understand:

- the proportion of all young people who go on to higher education

- lifestyle patterns of children and young people (e.g. pocket money, leaving home on reaching adulthood)

- changing family patterns and attitudes to changing family patterns (e.g. divorce)

- that education in Britain is free and compulsory, and that there is compulsory testing (in England and Scotland) at ages 7, 11 and 14; there are also GSCE and/or vocational exams at 16; and Advanced level exams (A and AS) at ages 17 and 18

- that there are strict laws regarding the employment of children

- that there are important health concerns and laws relating to children and young people and smoking, alcohol and drugs, and

- that young people are eligible to vote in elections from age 18.

The nations and regions of the UK

The UK is a medium-sized country. The longest distance on the mainland, from John O'Groats on the north coast of Scotland to Land's End in the south-west corner of England, is about 870 miles (approximately 1,400 kilometres). Most of the population live in towns and cities.

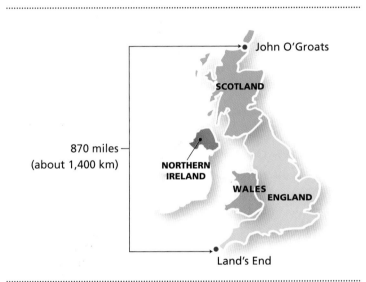

There are many variations in culture and language in the different parts of the United Kingdom. This is seen in differences in architecture, in some local customs, in types of food, and especially in language. The English language has many accents and dialects. These are a clear indication of regional differences in the UK. Well-known dialects in England are Geordie (Tyneside), Scouse (Liverpool) and Cockney (London). Many other languages in addition to English are spoken in the UK, especially in multicultural cities.

In Wales, Scotland and Northern Ireland, people speak different varieties and dialects of English. In Wales, too, an increasing number of people speak Welsh, which is taught in schools and universities. In Scotland Gaelic is spoken in some parts of the Highlands and Islands and in Northern Ireland a few people speak Irish Gaelic. Some of the dialects of English spoken in Scotland show the influence of the old Scottish language, Scots. One of the dialects spoken in Northern Ireland is called Ulster Scots.

Religion

> The 2011 Census results are due in 2012, and will differ from the facts shown here. However, for the purposes of your test you must learn the text as based on the 2001 Census.

Although the UK is historically a Christian society, everyone has the legal right to practise the religion of their choice. In the 2001 census, just over 75% said they had a religion: 7 out of 10 of these were Christians. There were also a considerable number of people who followed other religions. Although many people in the UK said they held religious beliefs, currently only around 10% of the population attend religious services. More people attend services in Scotland and Northern Ireland than in England and Wales. In London the number of people who attend religious services is increasing.

Religions in the UK

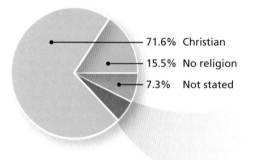

71.6% Christian
15.5% No religion
7.3%   Not stated

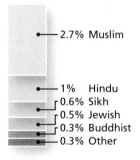

2.7% Muslim

1%   Hindu
0.6% Sikh
0.5% Jewish
0.3% Buddhist
0.3% Other

Source: National Statistics from the 2001 census

1. Christian*	71.6%
2. Muslim	2.7%
3. Hindu	1.0%
4. Sikh	0.6%
5. Jewish	0.5%
6. Buddhist	0.3%
Other	0.3%
Total all	**77.0%**
No religion	15.5%
Not stated	7.3%

* 10% of whom are Roman Catholic

THE CHRISTIAN CHURCHES

In England there is a constitutional link between church and state. The official church of the state is the Church of England. The Church of England is called the Anglican Church in other countries and the Episcopal Church in Scotland and in the USA. The Church of England is a Protestant church and has existed since the Reformation in the 1530s. The King or Queen (the monarch) is the head, or Supreme Governor, of the Church of England. The monarch is not allowed to marry anyone who is not Protestant. The spiritual leader of the Church of England is the Archbishop of Canterbury. The monarch has the right to select the Archbishop and other senior church officials, but usually the choice is made by the Prime Minister and a committee appointed by the Church. Several Church of England bishops sit in the House of Lords (see **Chapter 4**). The Church of Scotland is Presbyterian, national and free from state control. It has no bishops and is governed for spiritual purposes by a series of courts, so its most senior representative is the Moderator (chairperson) of its annual General Assembly. There is no established church in Wales or in Northern Ireland.

Other Protestant Christian groups in the UK are Baptists, Presbyterians, Methodists and Quakers. 10% of Christians are Roman Catholic (40% in Northern Ireland).

> " The Church of England is a Protestant church and has existed since the Reformation in the 1530s. The King or Queen (the monarch) is the head, or Supreme Governor, of the Church of England. "

✓ Check that you understand:

- the percentage of the UK population that say they are Christian

- how many people say they have no religion

- what percentage are Muslim, Hindu, Sikh, Jewish or Buddhist

- everyone in the UK has the right to practise their religion

- the Anglican Church, or Church of England, is the church of the state in England (established church)

- the monarch (King or Queen) is head of the Church of England

- in Scotland the established church is the Presbyterian Church of Scotland. In Wales and Northern Ireland there is no established church, and

- the difference between the Church of Scotland and the Church of England in Scotland.

Patron saints

England, Scotland, Wales and Northern Ireland each have a national saint called a patron saint. Each saint has a feast day. In the past these were celebrated as holy days when many people had a day off work. Today these are not public holidays except for 17 March in Northern Ireland.

Patron saints' days

St Patrick's Day is a bank holiday in Northern Ireland, not a public holiday. However, for the purposes of your test you must learn the text as reproduced here.

St David's Day	Wales	1 March
St Patrick's Day	Northern Ireland	17 March
St George's Day	England	23 April
St Andrew's Day	Scotland	30 November

There are four 'bank holidays' and four other public holidays a year (most people call all these holidays bank holidays).

Customs and traditions

FESTIVALS

Throughout the year there are festivals of art, music and culture, such as the Notting Hill Carnival in west London and the Edinburgh Festival. Customs and traditions from various religions, such as Eid ul-Fitr (Muslim), Diwali (Hindu) and Hanukkah (Jewish) are widely recognised in the UK. Children learn about these at school. The main Christian festivals are Christmas and Easter. There are also celebrations of non-religious traditions such as New Year.

THE MAIN CHRISTIAN FESTIVALS

Christmas Day

25 December celebrates the birth of Jesus Christ. It is a public holiday. Many Christians go to church on Christmas Eve (24 December) or on Christmas Day itself. Christmas is also usually celebrated by people who are not Christian. People usually spend the day at home and eat a special meal, which often includes turkey. They give each other gifts, send each other cards and decorate their houses. Many people decorate a tree. Christmas is a special time for children. Very young children believe that an old man, Father Christmas (or Santa Claus), brings them presents during the night. He is always shown in pictures with a long white beard, dressed in red. Boxing Day, 26 December, is the day after Christmas. It is a public holiday.

> Customs and traditions from various religions, such as Eid ul-Fitr (Muslim), Diwali (Hindu) and Hanukkah (Jewish) are widely recognised in the UK. Children learn about these at school.

OTHER FESTIVALS AND TRADITIONS

New Year

1 January is a public holiday. People usually celebrate on the night of 31 December. In Scotland, 31 December is called Hogmanay and 2 January is also a public holiday. In Scotland Hogmanay is a bigger holiday for some people than Christmas.

Valentine's Day

14 February is when lovers exchange cards and gifts. Sometimes people send anonymous cards to someone they secretly admire.

April Fool's Day

1 April is a day when people play jokes on each other until midday.

Often TV and newspapers carry stories intended to deceive credulous viewers and readers.

Mother's Day

The Sunday three weeks before Easter is a day when children send cards or buy gifts for their mothers. Easter is also an important Christian festival.

Halloween

31 October is a very ancient festival. Young people will often dress up in frightening costumes to play 'trick or treat'. Giving them sweets or chocolates might stop them playing a trick on you. Sometimes people carry lanterns made out of pumpkins with a candle inside.

Guy Fawkes Night

5 November is an occasion when people in Great Britain set off fireworks at home or in special displays. The origin of this celebration was an event in 1605, when a group of Catholics led by Guy Fawkes failed in their plan to kill the Protestant King with a bomb in the Houses of Parliament.

Remembrance Day

11 November commemorates those who died fighting in the First World War, the Second World War and other wars. Many people wear poppies (a red flower) in memory of those who died. At 11am, there is a two-minute silence.

SPORT

Northern Ireland don't have a national rugby team, but they do have a national football team. However, for the purposes of your test you must learn the text as reproduced here.

Sport of all kinds plays an important part in many people's lives. Football, tennis, rugby and cricket are very popular sports in the UK. There are no United Kingdom teams for football and rugby. England, Scotland, Wales and Northern Ireland have their own teams. Important sporting events include the Grand National horse race, the Football Association (FA) cup final (and equivalents in Northern Ireland, Scotland and Wales), the Open golf championship and the Wimbledon tennis tournament.

Check that you understand:

- which sports are most popular in the UK
- the patron saints' days in England, Scotland, Wales and Northern Ireland
- what bank holidays are
- the main traditional festivals in the UK, and
- that the main festivals in the UK are Christian-based, but that important festivals from other religions are recognised and explained to children in schools.

CHAPTER 4
How the United Kingdom is Governed

➜ IN THIS CHAPTER you will learn the basic elements of how government in Britain works. The UK is unusual as it does not have a written constitution. Britain uses institutions, as well as conventions and traditions, to provide the guidance usually delivered by a written constitution. The chapter focuses on these institutions and how they work together to provide fair and good government. You need to focus on how each institution operates. You will also learn about the ways the government has passed some of its powers down to other institutions, known as devolved administration.

In addition, you will learn about the political rights enjoyed by every UK citizen, such as voting. Finally, the chapter looks at Britain's role in the world and in Europe. It discusses the Commonwealth, the European Union and the United Nations. You should focus on the UK's gradual move into closer co-operation with its European neighbours. Make sure you understand the crucial role that the European Union has in Britain.

IN THIS CHAPTER THERE IS INFORMATION ABOUT:

- The system of government
- The monarchy
- The electoral system
- Political parties
- Being a citizen
- Voting
- Contacting your MP
- The UK in Europe and the world
- The European Union
- The Commonwealth
- The United Nations

The British constitution

As a constitutional democracy, the United Kingdom is governed by a wide range of institutions, many of which provide checks on each other's powers. Most of these institutions are of long standing: they include the monarchy, parliament (consisting of the House of Commons and the House of Lords), the office of Prime Minister, the Cabinet, the judiciary, the police, the civil service and the institutions of local government. More recently, devolved administrations have been set up for Scotland, Wales and Northern Ireland. Together, these formal institutions, laws and conventions form the British constitution. Some people would argue that the roles of other less formal institutions, such as the media and pressure groups, should also be seen as part of the constitution.

> The British constitution is not written down in any single document, as are the constitutions of many other countries.

The British constitution is not written down in any single document, as are the constitutions of many other countries. This is mainly because the United Kingdom has never had a lasting revolution, like America or France, so our most important institutions have been in existence for hundreds of years. Some people believe that there should be a single document, but others believe that an unwritten constitution allows more scope for institutions to adapt to meet changing circumstances and public expectations.

THE MONARCHY

Queen Elizabeth II is the Head of State of the United Kingdom. She is also the monarch or Head of State for many countries in the Commonwealth. The UK, like Denmark, the Netherlands, Norway, Spain and Sweden, has a constitutional monarchy. This means that the King or Queen does not rule the country, but appoints the government which the people have chosen in democratic elections. Although the Queen or King can advise, warn and encourage the Prime Minister, the decisions on government policies are made by the Prime Minister and Cabinet.

The Queen has reigned since her father's death in 1952. Prince Charles, the Prince of Wales, her oldest son, is the heir to the throne.

The Queen has important ceremonial roles such as the opening of the new parliamentary session each year. On this occasion the Queen makes a speech that summarises the government's policies for the year ahead.

GOVERNMENT

The system of government in the United Kingdom is a parliamentary democracy. The UK is divided into 646 parliamentary constituencies and at least every five years voters in each constituency elect their Member of Parliament (MP) in a general election. All of the elected MPs form the House of Commons. Most MPs belong to a political party and the party with the largest number of MPs forms the government.

The law that requires new elections to parliament to be held at least every five years is so fundamental that no government has sought to change it. A Bill to change it is the only one to which the House of Lords must give its consent.

Some people argue that the power of parliament is lessened because of the obligation on the United Kingdom to accept the rules of the European Union and the judgments of the European Court, but it was parliament itself which created these obligations.

Following the general election in 2010 there are now 650 constituencies in the UK. However, for the purposes of your test you must learn the text as reproduced here.

THE HOUSE OF COMMONS

The House of Commons is the more important of the two chambers in parliament, and its members are democratically elected. Nowadays the Prime Minister and almost all the members of the Cabinet are members of the House of Commons. The members of the House of Commons are called Members of Parliament or MPs for short. Each MP represents a parliamentary constituency, or area of the country: there are 646 of these. MPs have a number of different responsibilities. They represent everyone in their constituency, they help to create new laws, they scrutinise and comment on what the government is doing, and they debate important national issues.

ELECTIONS

There must be a general election to elect MPs at least every five years, though they may be held sooner if the Prime Minister so decides. If an MP dies or resigns, there will be another election, called a by-election, in his or her constituency. MPs are elected through a system called 'first past the post'. In each constituency, the candidate who gets the most votes is elected. The government is then formed by the party which wins the majority of constituencies.

"There must be a general election to elect MPs at least every five years, though they may be held sooner if the Prime Minister so decides."

THE WHIPS

The Whips are a small group of MPs appointed by their party leaders. They are responsible for discipline in their party and making sure MPs attend the House of Commons to vote. The Chief Whip often attends Cabinet or Shadow Cabinet meetings and arranges the schedule of proceedings in the House of Commons with the Speaker.

EUROPEAN PARLIAMENTARY ELECTIONS

Elections for the European Parliament are also held every five years. There are 78 seats for representatives from the UK in the European Parliament and elected members are called Members of the European Parliament (MEPs). Elections to the European Parliament use a system of proportional representation, whereby seats are allocated to each party in proportion to the total votes it won.

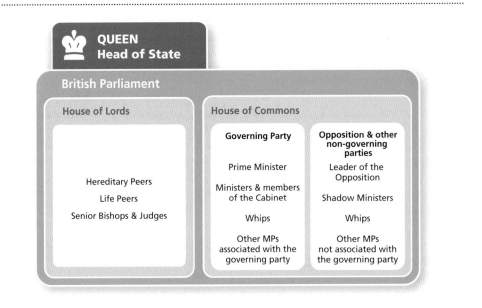

THE HOUSE OF LORDS

Members of the House of Lords, known as peers, are not elected and do not represent a constituency. The role and membership of the House of Lords have recently undergone big changes. Until

1958 all peers were either 'hereditary', meaning that their titles were inherited, senior judges, or bishops of the Church of England. Since 1958 the Prime Minister has had the power to appoint peers just for their own lifetime. These peers, known as Life Peers, have usually had a distinguished career in politics, business, law or some other profession. This means that debates in the House of Lords often draw on more specialist knowledge than is available to members of the House of Commons. Life Peers are appointed by the Queen on the advice of the Prime Minister, but they include people nominated by the leaders of the other main parties and by an independent Appointments Commission for non-party peers.

In the last few years the hereditary peers have lost the automatic right to attend the House of Lords, although they are allowed to elect a few of their number to represent them.

While the House of Lords is usually the less important of the two chambers of parliament, it is more independent of the government. It can suggest amendments or propose new laws, which are then discussed by the House of Commons. The House of Lords can become very important if the majority of its members will not agree to pass a law for which the House of Commons has voted. The House of Commons has powers to overrule the House of Lords, but these are very rarely used.

> Whilst Life Peers are selected by the Prime Minister, or other MPs and peers, the Queen formally appoints them to their position.

THE PRIME MINISTER

The Prime Minister (PM) is the leader of the political party in power. He or she appoints the members of the Cabinet and has control over many important public appointments. The official home of the Prime Minister is 10 Downing Street, in central London, near the Houses of Parliament; he or she also has a country house not far from London called Chequers. The Prime Minister can be changed if the MPs in the governing party decide to do so, or if he or she wishes to resign. More usually, the Prime Minister resigns when his or her party is defeated in a general election.

THE CABINET

The Prime Minister appoints about 20 senior MPs to become ministers in charge of departments. These include the Chancellor of the Exchequer, responsible for the economy, the Home Secretary, responsible for law, order and immigration, the Foreign Secretary, and ministers (called Secretaries of State) for education, health and defence. The Lord Chancellor, who is the minister

> The Prime Minister appoints about 20 senior MPs to become ministers in charge of departments. These ministers form the Cabinet, a small committee which usually meets weekly.

responsible for legal affairs, is also a member of the Cabinet but sat in the House of Lords rather than the House of Commons. Following legislation passed in 2005, it is now possible for the Lord Chancellor to sit in the Commons. These ministers form the Cabinet, a small committee which usually meets weekly and makes important decisions about government policy which often then have to be debated or approved by parliament.

THE OPPOSITION

The second largest party in the House of Commons is called the Opposition. The Leader of the Opposition is the person who hopes to become Prime Minister if his or her party wins the next general election. The Leader of the Opposition leads his or her party in pointing out the government's failures and weaknesses; one important opportunity to do this is at Prime Minister's Questions which takes place every week while parliament is sitting. The Leader of the Opposition also appoints senior Opposition MPs to lead the criticism of government ministers, and together they form the Shadow Cabinet.

> **The Speaker is politically neutral. He or she is an MP, elected by fellow MPs to keep order during political debates and to make sure the rules are followed.**

THE SPEAKER

Debates in the House of Commons are chaired by the Speaker, the chief officer of the House of Commons. The Speaker is politically neutral. He or she is an MP, elected by fellow MPs to keep order during political debates and to make sure the rules are followed. This includes making sure the Opposition has a guaranteed amount of time to debate issues it chooses. The Speaker also represents parliament at ceremonial occasions.

THE PARTY SYSTEM

Under the British system of parliamentary democracy, anyone can stand for election as an MP but they are unlikely to win an election unless they have been nominated to represent one of the major political parties. These are the Labour Party, the Conservative Party, the Liberal Democrats, or one of the parties representing Scottish, Welsh or Northern Irish interests. There are just a few MPs who do not represent any of the main political parties, and are called 'independents'. The main political parties actively seek members among ordinary voters to join their debates, contribute to their costs and help at elections for parliament or for local government; they have branches in most constituencies and they hold policy-making conferences every year.

PRESSURE AND LOBBY GROUPS

Pressure and lobby groups are organisations that try to influence government policy. They play a very important role in politics. There are many pressure groups in the UK. They may represent economic interests (such as the Confederation of British Industry, the Consumers' Association or the trade unions) or views on particular subjects (e.g. Greenpeace or Liberty). The general public is more likely to support pressure groups than join a political party.

THE CIVIL SERVICE

Civil servants are managers and administrators who carry out government policy. They have to be politically neutral and professional, regardless of which political party is in power. Although civil servants have to follow the policies of the elected government, they can warn ministers if they think a policy is impractical or not in the public interest. Before a general election takes place, top civil servants study the Opposition party's policies closely in case they need to be ready to serve a new government with different aims and policies.

DEVOLVED ADMINISTRATION

In order to give people in Wales and Scotland more control of matters that directly affect them, in 1997 the government began a programme of devolving power from central government. Since 1999 there has been a Welsh Assembly, a Scottish Parliament and, periodically, a Northern Ireland Assembly. Although policy and laws governing defence, foreign affairs, taxation and social security all remain under central UK Government control, many other public services now come under the control of the devolved administrations in Wales and Scotland.

Both the Scottish Parliament and Welsh Assembly have been set up using forms of proportional representation, which ensures that each party gets a number of seats in proportion to the number of votes they receive. Similarly, proportional representation is used in Northern Ireland in order to ensure 'power sharing' between the Unionist majority (mainly Protestant) and the substantial (mainly Catholic) minority aligned to Irish nationalist parties. A different form of proportional representation is used for elections to the European Parliament.

> **"** ... policy and laws governing defence, foreign affairs, taxation and social security all remain under central UK Government control ... **"**

THE WELSH ASSEMBLY GOVERNMENT

The National Assembly for Wales, or Welsh Assembly Government (WAG), is situated in Cardiff, the capital city of Wales. It has 60 Assembly Members (AMs) and elections are held every four years. Members can speak in either Welsh or English and all its publications are in both languages. The Assembly has the power to make decisions on important matters such as education policy, the environment, health services, transport and local government, and to pass laws for Wales on these matters within a statutory framework set out by the UK Parliament at Westminster.

" The matters on which the Scottish Parliament can legislate include civil and criminal law, health, education, planning and the raising of additional taxes. **"**

THE PARLIAMENT OF SCOTLAND

A long campaign in Scotland for more independence and democratic control led to the formation in 1999 of the Parliament of Scotland, which sits in Edinburgh, the capital city of Scotland.

There are 129 Members of the Scottish Parliament (MSPs), elected by a form of proportional representation. This has led to the sharing of power in Scotland between the Labour and Liberal Democrat parties. The Scottish Parliament can pass legislation for Scotland on all matters that are not specifically reserved to the UK Parliament. The matters on which the Scottish Parliament can legislate include civil and criminal law, health, education, planning and the raising of additional taxes.

THE NORTHERN IRELAND ASSEMBLY

A Northern Ireland Parliament was established in 1922 when Ireland was divided, but it was abolished in 1972 shortly after the Troubles broke out in 1969.

Soon after the end of the Troubles, the Northern Ireland Assembly was established with a power-sharing agreement which distributes ministerial offices among the main parties. The Assembly has 108 elected members known as MLAs (Members of the Legislative Assembly). Decision-making powers devolved to Northern Ireland include education, agriculture, the environment, health and social services in Northern Ireland.

The Northern Ireland Assembly was reinstated in 2007. However, for the purposes of your test you must learn the text as reproduced here.

The UK Government kept the power to suspend the Northern Ireland Assembly if the political leaders no longer agreed to work together or if the Assembly was not working in the interests of the people of Northern Ireland. This has happened several times and the Assembly is currently suspended (2006). This means that the elected assembly members do not have power to pass bills or make decisions.

LOCAL GOVERNMENT

Towns, cities and rural areas in the UK are governed by democratically elected councils, often called local authorities. Some areas have both district and county councils which have different functions, although most larger towns and cities will have a single local authority. Many councils representing towns and cities appoint a mayor who is the ceremonial leader of the council but in some towns a mayor is appointed to be the effective leader of the administration. London has 33 local authorities, with the Greater London Authority and the Mayor of London co-ordinating policies across the capital. Local authorities are required to provide 'mandatory services' in their area. These services include education, housing, social services, passenger transport, the fire service, rubbish collection, planning, environmental health and libraries.

Most of the money for the local authority services comes from the government through taxes. Only about 20% is funded locally through 'council tax', a local tax set by councils to help pay for local services. It applies to all domestic properties, including houses, bungalows, flats, maisonettes, mobile homes or houseboats, whether owned or rented.

Local elections for councillors are held in May every year. Many candidates stand for council election as members of a political party.

THE JUDICIARY

In the UK the laws made by parliament are the highest authority. But often important questions arise about how the laws are to be interpreted in particular cases. It is the task of the judges (who are together called 'the judiciary') to interpret the law, and the government may not interfere with their role. Often the actions of the government are claimed to be illegal and, if the judges agree, then the government must either change its policies or ask parliament to change the law. This has become all the more important in recent years, as the judges now have the task of applying the Human Rights Act. If they find that a public body is not respecting a person's human rights, they may order that body to change its practices and to pay compensation, if appropriate. If

> **Most of the money for the local authority services comes from the government through taxes. Only about 20% is funded locally through 'council tax'.**

the judges believe that an Act of Parliament is incompatible with the Human Rights Act, they cannot change it themselves but they can ask parliament to consider doing so.

Judges cannot, however, decide whether people are guilty or innocent of serious crimes. When someone is accused of a serious crime, a jury will decide whether he or she is innocent or guilty and, if guilty, the judge will decide on the penalty. For less important crimes, a magistrate will decide on guilt and on any penalty.

THE POLICE

> **The police have 'operational independence', which means that the government cannot instruct them on what to do in any particular case.**

The police service is organised locally, with one police service for each county or group of counties. The largest force is the Metropolitan Police, which serves London and is based at New Scotland Yard. Northern Ireland as a whole is served by the Police Service for Northern Ireland (PSNI). The police have 'operational independence', which means that the government cannot instruct them on what to do in any particular case. But the powers of the police are limited by the law and their finances are controlled by the government and by police authorities made up of councillors and magistrates. The Independent Police Complaints Commission (or, in Northern Ireland, the Police Ombudsman) investigates serious complaints against the police.

NON-DEPARTMENTAL PUBLIC BODIES (QUANGOS)

Non-departmental public bodies, also known as quangos, are independent organisations that carry out functions on behalf of the public which it would be inappropriate to place under the political control of a Cabinet minister. There are many hundreds of these bodies, carrying out a wide variety of public duties. Appointments to these bodies are usually made by ministers, but they must do so in an open and fair way.

Watch & Learn:

www.lifeintheuk.net/2012ec3

Scan to watch videos which help explain how Parliament works.

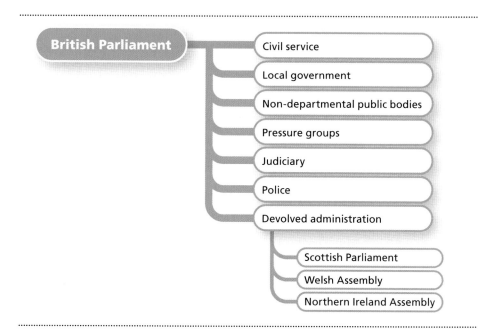

THE ROLE OF THE MEDIA

Proceedings in parliament are broadcast on digital television and published in official reports such as Hansard, which is available in large libraries and on the internet: www.parliament.uk. Most people, however, get information about political issues and events from newspapers (often called the press), television and radio.

The UK has a free press, meaning that what is written in newspapers is free from government control. Newspaper owners and editors hold strong political opinions and run campaigns to try and influence government policy and public opinion. As a result it is sometimes difficult to distinguish fact from opinion in newspaper coverage.

By law, radio and television coverage of the political parties at election periods must be balanced and so equal time has to be given to rival viewpoints. But broadcasters are free to interview politicians in a tough and lively way.

> Proceedings in parliament are broadcast on digital television and published in official reports such as Hansard, which is available in large libraries and on the internet.

WHO CAN VOTE?

The United Kingdom has had a fully democratic system since 1928, when women were allowed to vote at 21, the same age as men.

The present voting age of 18 was set in 1969, and (with a few exceptions such as convicted prisoners) all UK-born and naturalised citizens have full civic rights, including the right to vote and do jury service.

Citizens of the UK, and the Commonwealth and the Irish Republic (if resident in the UK) can vote in all public elections. Citizens of EU states who are resident in the UK can vote in all elections except national parliamentary (general) elections.

In order to vote in a parliamentary, local or European election, you must have your name on the register of electors, known as the electoral register. If you are eligible to vote, you can register by contacting your local council election registration office. If you don't know what your local authority is, you can find out by telephoning the Local Government Association (LGA) information line on 020 7664 3131 between 9am and 5pm, Monday to Friday. You will have to tell them your postcode or your full address and they will be able to give you the name of your local authority. You can also get voter registration forms in English, Welsh and some other languages on the internet: www.electoralcommission.org.uk

> "Citizens of the UK, and the Commonwealth and the Irish Republic (if resident in the UK) can vote in all public elections."

The electoral register is updated every year in September or October. An electoral registration form is sent to every household and it has to be completed and returned, with the names of everyone who is resident in the household and eligible to vote on 15 October.

In Northern Ireland a different system operates. This is called individual registration and all those entitled to vote must complete their own registration form. Once registered, you can stay on the register provided your personal details do not change. For more information telephone the Electoral Office for Northern Ireland on 028 9044 6688.

By law, each local authority has to make its electoral register available for anyone to look at, although this now has to be supervised. The register is kept at each local electoral registration office (or council office in England and Wales). It is also possible to see the register at some public buildings such as libraries.

STANDING FOR OFFICE

Most citizens of the United Kingdom, the Irish Republic or the Commonwealth aged 18 or over can stand for public office. There are some exceptions and these include members of the armed forces, civil servants and people found guilty of certain criminal offences. Members of the House of Lords may not stand for election to the House of Commons but are eligible for all other public offices.

To become a local councillor, a candidate must have a local connection with the area through work, being on the electoral register, or through renting or owning land or property.

CONTACTING ELECTED MEMBERS

All elected members have a duty to serve and represent their constituents. You can get contact details for all your representatives and their parties from your local library. Assembly members, MSPs, MPs and MEPs are also listed in the phone book and Yellow Pages. You can contact MPs by letter or phone at their constituency office or their office in the House of Commons. The House of Commons, Westminster, London SW1A 0AA, or telephone: 020 7729 3000. Many Assembly Members, MSPs, MPs and MEPs hold regular local 'surgeries'. These are often advertised in the local paper and constituents can go and talk about issues in person. You can find out the name of your local MP and get in touch with them by fax through the website: www.writetothem.com. This service is free.

HOW TO VISIT PARLIAMENT AND THE DEVOLVED ADMINISTRATIONS

The public can listen to debates in the Palace of Westminster from public galleries in both the House of Commons and the House of Lords. You can either write to your local MP in advance to ask for tickets or you can queue on the day at the public entrance. Entrance is free. Sometimes there are long queues for the House of Commons and you may have to wait for at least one or two hours. It is usually easier to get into the House of Lords. You can find further information on the UK Parliament website: www.parliament.uk

In Northern Ireland, elected members, known as MLAs, meet in the Northern Ireland Assembly at Stormont, in Belfast. The Northern Ireland Assembly is presently suspended. There are two ways to arrange a visit to Stormont. You can either contact the Education Service (details on the Northern Ireland Assembly website: www.niassembly.gov.uk) or contact an MLA.

The public can listen to debates in the Palace of Westminster from public galleries in both the House of Commons and the House of Lords. You can either write to your local MP in advance to ask for tickets or you can queue on the day.

In Scotland, the elected members, called MSPs, meet in the Scottish Parliament at Holyrood in Edinburgh (for more information see: www.scottish.parliament.uk). You can get information, book tickets or arrange tours through the visitor services. You can write to them at The Scottish Parliament, Edinburgh, EH99 1SP or telephone: 0131 348 5200, or email sp.bookings@scottish.parliament.uk

In Wales, the elected members, known as AMs, meet in the Welsh Assembly in the Senedd in Cardiff Bay (for more information see: www.wales.gov.uk). You can book guided tours or seats in the public galleries for the Welsh Assembly. To make a booking, telephone the Assembly booking line on 029 2089 8477 or email: assembly.booking@wales.gsi.gov.uk

✓ **Check that you understand:**

- the role of the monarchy
- how parliament works, and the difference between the House of Commons and the House of Lords
- how often general elections are held
- where the official residence of the Prime Minister is
- the role of the Cabinet and who is in it
- the nature of the UK constitution
- the job of the Opposition, the Leader of the Opposition and the Shadow Cabinet
- the difference between 'first past the post' and proportional representation
- the form of electoral systems in the devolved administrations in Northern Ireland, Scotland and Wales
- the rights and duties of British citizens, including naturalised citizens
- how the judiciary, police and local authorities work, and
- what non-departmental public bodies are.

The UK in Europe and the world

THE COMMONWEALTH

The Commonwealth is an association of countries, most of which were once part of the British Empire, though a few countries that were not in the Empire have also joined it.

Commonwealth members

- Antigua and Barbuda
- Australia
- The Bahamas
- Bangladesh
- Barbados
- Belize
- Botswana
- Brunei Darussalam
- Cameroon
- Canada
- Cyprus
- Dominica
- Fiji Islands
- The Gambia
- Ghana
- Grenada
- Guyana
- India
- Jamaica
- Kenya
- Kiribati
- Lesotho
- Malawi
- Malaysia
- Maldives
- Malta
- Mauritius
- Mozambique
- Namibia
- Nauru*
- New Zealand
- Nigeria
- Pakistan
- Papua New Guinea
- St Kitts and Nevis
- St Lucia
- St Vincent and the Grenadines
- Samoa
- Seychelles
- Sierra Leone
- Singapore
- Solomon Islands
- South Africa
- Sri Lanka
- Swaziland
- Tonga
- Trinidad and Tobago
- Tuvalu
- Uganda
- United Kingdom
- United Republic of Tanzania
- Vanuatu
- Zambia

* Nauru is a Special Member.

There are now 54 countries in the Commonwealth, as Rwanda joined in 2009. However, for the purposes of your test you must learn the text as reproduced here.

Romania and Bulgaria joined the EU in 2007, not 2006. However, for the purposes of your test you must learn the text as reproduced here.

66

One of the main aims of the EU today is for member states to function as a single market.

99

The Queen is the head of the Commonwealth, which currently has 53 member states. Membership is voluntary and the Commonwealth has no power over its members although it can suspend membership. The Commonwealth aims to promote democracy, good government and to eradicate poverty.

THE EUROPEAN UNION (EU)

The European Union (EU), originally called the European Economic Community (EEC), was set up by six Western European countries who signed the Treaty of Rome on 25 March 1957. One of the main reasons for doing this was the belief that co-operation between states would reduce the likelihood of another war in Europe. Originally the UK decided not to join this group and only became part of the European Union in 1973. In 2004 ten new member countries joined the EU, with a further two in 2006 making a total of 27 member countries.

One of the main aims of the EU today is for member states to function as a single market. Most of the countries of the EU have a shared currency, the euro, but the UK has decided to retain its own currency unless the British people choose to accept the euro in a referendum. Citizens of an EU member state have the right to travel to and work in any EU country if they have a valid passport or identity card. This right can be restricted on the grounds of public health, public order and public security. The right to work is also sometimes restricted for citizens of countries that have joined the EU recently.

The Council of the European Union (usually called the Council of Ministers) is effectively the governing body of the EU. It is made up of government ministers from each country in the EU and, together with the European Parliament, is the legislative body of the EU. The Council of Ministers passes EU law on the recommendations of the European Commission and the European Parliament and takes the most important decisions about how the EU is run. The European Commission is based in Brussels, the capital city of Belgium. It is the civil service of the EU and drafts proposals for new EU policies and laws and administers its funding programmes.

The European Parliament meets in Strasbourg, in north-eastern France, and in Brussels. Each country elects members, called Members of the European Parliament (MEPs), every five years. The European Parliament examines decisions made by the European Council and the European Commission, and it has the power to

Institutions of the European Union

European Commission

- The civil service of the EU
- Drafts proposals for new EU policies and laws
- Administers EU funding programmes

Legislature

Council of Ministers
(also known as the Council of the European Union)

- Passes EU law on the recommendations of the European Commission and the European Parliament
- Takes the most important decisions about how the EU is run
- Made up of government ministers from each country in the EU

European Parliament

- Made up of elected members (MEPs) from each country in the EU
- Examines decisions made by the European Commission
- Can refuse agreement to European laws proposed by the Commission
- Checks on the spending of EU funds

refuse agreement to European laws proposed by the Commission and to check on the spending of EU funds.

European Union law is legally binding in the UK and all the other member states. European laws, called directives, regulations or framework decisions, have made a lot of difference to people's rights in the UK, particularly at work. For example, there are EU directives about the procedures for making workers redundant, and regulations that limit the number of hours people can be made to work.

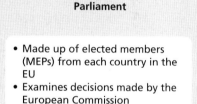

"
European Union law is legally binding in the UK and all the other member states.
"

THE COUNCIL OF EUROPE

The Council of Europe was created in 1949 and the UK was one of the founder members. Most of the countries of Europe are members. It has no power to make laws but draws up conventions and charters which focus on human rights, democracy, education, the environment, health and culture. The most important of these is the European Convention on Human Rights; all member states are bound by this Convention and a member state which persistently refuses to obey the Convention may be expelled from the Council of Europe.

THE UNITED NATIONS (UN)

The UK is a member of the United Nations (UN), an international organisation to which over 190 countries now belong. The UN was set up after the Second World War and aims to prevent war and promote international peace and security. There are 15 members on the UN Security Council, which recommends action by the UN when there are international crises and threats to peace. The UK is one of the five permanent members.

Three very important agreements produced by the UN are the Universal Declaration of Human Rights, the Convention on the Elimination of All Forms of Discrimination against Women, and the UN Convention on the Rights of the Child. Although none of these has the force of law, they are widely used in political debate and legal cases to reinforce the law and to assess the behaviour of countries.

✓ Check that you understand:

- the differences between the Council of Europe, the European Union, the European Commission and the European Parliament
- the UK's relationship with the Council of Europe and the European Union
- that the EU aims to become a single market and it is administered by a Council of Ministers of governments of member states
- the rights of EU citizens to travel and work in EU countries, and
- the roles of the UN and the Commonwealth.

Watch & Learn:

www.lifeintheuk.net/2012ec4

Scan to watch a video which clearly explains everything you need to know about the EU.

CHAPTER 5
Everyday Needs

→ IN THIS CHAPTER you will learn about some of the key services and activities integral to everyday life in Britain. Many of these services are provided by the government and others are delivered by private companies. It is important to understand the legal and other rights you have when receiving services, but also the obligations you have to meet such as taxes and other costs for services. Government services such as healthcare and education are delivered by various agencies, and vary between the regions of the UK. You should also focus on the detailed rules and regulations that govern many everyday activities.

IN THIS CHAPTER THERE IS INFORMATION ABOUT:

- Housing
- Services in and for the home
- Money and credit
- Health
- Pregnancy and care of the young
- Education
- Leisure
- Travel and transport
- Identity documents

Housing

BUYING A HOME

Two-thirds of people in the UK own their own home. Most other people rent houses, flats or rooms.

MORTGAGES

People who buy their own home usually pay for it with a mortgage, a special loan from a bank or building society. This loan is paid back, with interest, over a long period of time, usually 25 years. You can get information about mortgages from a bank or building society. Some banks can also give information about Islamic (Sharia) mortgages.

If you are having problems paying your mortgage repayments, you can get help and advice (see **Help** section later in this chapter). It is important to speak to your bank or building society as soon as you can.

> People who buy their own home usually pay for it with a mortgage, a special loan from a bank or building society. This loan is paid back, with interest, over a long period of time, usually 25 years.

ESTATE AGENTS

If you wish to buy a home, usually the first place to start is an estate agent. In Scotland the process is different and you should go first to a solicitor. Estate agents represent the person selling their house or flat. They arrange for buyers to visit homes that are for sale. There are estate agents in all towns and cities and they usually have websites where they advertise the homes for sale. You can also find details about homes for sale on the internet and in national and local newspapers.

MAKING AN OFFER

In the UK, except in Scotland, when you find a home you wish to buy you have to make an offer to the seller. You usually do this through an estate agent or solicitor. Many people offer a lower price than the seller is asking. Your first offer must be 'subject to contract' so that you can withdraw if there are reasons why you cannot complete the purchase. In Scotland the seller sets a price and buyers make offers over that amount. The agreement becomes legally binding earlier than it does elsewhere in the UK.

SOLICITOR AND SURVEYOR

It is important that a solicitor helps you through the process of buying a house or flat. When you make an offer on a property, the solicitor will carry out a number of legal checks on the property, the seller and the local area. The solicitor will provide the legal agreements necessary for you to buy the property. The bank or building society that is providing you with your mortgage will also carry out checks on the house or flat you wish to buy. These are done by a surveyor. The buyer does not usually see the result of this survey, so the buyer often asks a second surveyor to check the house as well. In Scotland the survey is carried out before an offer is made, to help people decide how much they want to bid for the property.

RENTED ACCOMMODATION

It is possible to rent accommodation from the local authority (the council), from a housing association or from private property owners called landlords.

THE LOCAL AUTHORITY

Most local authorities (or councils) provide housing. This is often called 'council housing'. In Northern Ireland social housing is provided by the Northern Ireland Housing Executive (www.nihe.gov.uk). In Scotland you can find information on social housing at: www.sfha.co.uk. Everyone is entitled to apply for council accommodation. To apply you must put your name on the council register or list. This is available from the housing department at the local authority. You are then assessed according to your needs. This is done through a system of points. You get more points if you have priority needs, for example if you are homeless and have children or chronic ill health.

It is important to note that in many areas of the UK there is a shortage of council accommodation, and that some people have to wait a very long time for a house or flat.

HOUSING ASSOCIATIONS

Housing associations are independent not-for-profit organisations which provide housing for rent. In some areas they have taken over the administration of local authority housing. They also run schemes called shared ownership, which help people buy part of a

> " Housing associations are independent not-for-profit organisations which provide housing for rent. "

house or flat if they cannot afford to buy all of it at once. There are usually waiting lists for homes owned by housing associations.

PRIVATELY RENTED ACCOMMODATION

Many people rent houses or flats privately, from landlords. Information about private accommodation can be found in local newspapers, notice boards, estate agents and letting agents.

TENANCY AGREEMENT

When you rent a house or flat privately you sign a tenancy agreement, or lease. This explains the conditions or 'rules' you must follow while renting the property. This agreement must be checked very carefully to avoid problems later. The agreement also contains a list of any furniture or fittings in the property. This is called an inventory. Before you sign the agreement, check the details and keep it safe during your tenancy.

> "
> **You will probably be asked to give the landlord a deposit at the beginning of your tenancy. This is to cover the cost of any damage. It is usually equal to one month's rent.**
> "

DEPOSIT AND RENT

You will probably be asked to give the landlord a deposit at the beginning of your tenancy. This is to cover the cost of any damage. It is usually equal to one month's rent. The landlord must return this money to you at the end of your tenancy, unless you have caused damage to the property.

Your rent is fixed with your landlord at the beginning of the tenancy. The landlord cannot raise the rent without your agreement.

If you have a low income or are unemployed you may be able to claim Housing Benefit (see **Help**) to help you pay your rent.

RENEWING AND ENDING A TENANCY

Your tenancy agreement will be for a fixed period of time, often six months. After this time the tenancy can be ended or, if both tenant and landlord agree, renewed. If you end the tenancy before the fixed time, you usually have to pay the rent for the agreed full period of the tenancy.

A landlord cannot force a tenant to leave. If a landlord wishes a tenant to leave they must follow the correct procedures. These vary according to the type of tenancy. It is a criminal offence for a landlord to use threats or violence against a tenant or to force them to leave without an order from court.

DISCRIMINATION

It is unlawful for a landlord to discriminate against someone looking for accommodation because of their sex, race, nationality or ethnic group, or because they are disabled, unless the landlord or a close relative of the landlord is sharing the accommodation.

HOMELESSNESS

If you are homeless you should go for help to the local authority (or, in Northern Ireland, the Housing Executive). They have a legal duty to offer help and advice, but will not offer you a place to live unless you have priority need (see above) and have a connection with the area, such as work or family. You must also show that you have not made yourself intentionally homeless.

HELP

If you are homeless or have problems with your landlord, help can be found from the following:

- The housing department of the local authority will give advice on homelessness and on Housing Benefit as well as deal with problems you may have in council-owned property.

- The Citizens Advice Bureau will give advice on all types of housing problems. There may also be a housing advice centre in your neighbourhood.

- Shelter is a housing charity which runs a 24-hour helpline on 0808 800 4444, or visit www.shelternet.org.uk

- Help with the cost of moving and setting up home may be available from the Social Fund. This is run by the Department for Work and Pensions (DWP). It provides grants and loans such as the Community Care Grant for people setting up home after being homeless or after they have been in prison or other institutions. Other loans are available for people who have had an emergency such as flooding. Information about these is available at the Citizens Advice Bureau or Jobcentre Plus.

Services in and for the home

WATER

Water is supplied to all homes in the UK. The charge for this is called the water rates. When you move in to a new home (bought or rented), you should receive a letter telling you the name of the company responsible for supplying your water. The water rates may be paid in one payment (a lump sum) or in instalments, usually monthly. If you receive Housing Benefit, you should check to see if this covers the water rates. The cost of the water usually depends on the size of your property, but some homes have a water meter which tells you exactly how much water you have used. In Northern Ireland water is currently (2006) included in the domestic rates (see **Council tax**), although this may change in the future.

ELECTRICITY AND GAS

> All properties in the UK have electricity supplied at 240 volts. Most homes also have gas.

All properties in the UK have electricity supplied at 240 volts. Most homes also have gas. When you move into a new home or leave an old one, you should make a note of the electricity and gas meter readings. If you have an urgent problem with your gas, electricity or water supply, you can ring a 24-hour helpline. This can be found on your bill, in the Yellow Pages or in the phone book.

GAS AND ELECTRICITY SUPPLIERS

It is possible to choose between different gas and electricity suppliers. These have different prices and different terms and conditions. Get advice before you sign a contract with a new supplier. To find out which company supplies your gas, telephone Transco on 0870 608 1524.

To find out which company supplies your electricity, telephone Energywatch on 0845 906 0708 or visit: www.energywatch. org.uk. Energywatch can also give you advice on changing your supplier of electricity or gas.

TELEPHONE

Most homes already have a telephone line (called a land line). If you need a new line, telephone BT on 150 442, or contact a cable company. Many companies offer land line, mobile telephone and broadband internet services. You can get advice about prices or about changing your company from Ofcom at: www.ofcom.org.uk.

You can call from public payphones using cash, pre-paid phonecards or credit or debit cards. Calls made from hotels and hostels are usually more expensive. Dial 999 or 112 for emergency calls for police, fire or ambulance services. These calls are free. Do not use these numbers if it is not a real emergency; you can always find the local numbers for these services in the phone book.

BILLS

Information on how to pay for water, gas, electricity and the telephone is found on the back of each bill. If you have a bank account you can pay your bills by standing order or direct debit. Most companies operate a budget scheme which allows you to pay a fixed sum every month. If you do not pay a bill, the service can be cut off. To get a service reconnected, you have to pay another charge.

REFUSE COLLECTION

Refuse is also called waste, or rubbish. The local authority collects the waste regularly, usually on the same day of each week. Waste must be put outside in a particular place to get collected. In some parts of the country the waste is put into plastic bags, in others it is put into bins with wheels. In many places you must recycle your rubbish, separating paper, glass, metal or plastic from the other rubbish. Large objects which you want to throw away, such as a bed, a wardrobe or a fridge, need to be collected separately. Contact the local authority to arrange this. If you have a business, such as a factory or a shop, you must make special arrangements with the local authority for your waste to be collected. It is a criminal offence to dump rubbish anywhere.

COUNCIL TAX

Local government services, such as education, police, roads, refuse collection and libraries, are paid for partly by grants from the government and partly by council tax (see **Local government** in **Chapter 4**). In Northern Ireland there is a system of domestic rates instead of the council tax. The amount of council tax you pay depends on the size and value of your house or flat (dwelling).

> **"**
> If you have a bank account you can pay your bills by standing order or direct debit.
> **"**

You must register to pay council tax when you move into a new property, either as the owner or the tenant. You can pay the tax in one payment, in two instalments, or in ten instalments (from April to January).

If only one person lives in the flat or house, you get a 25% reduction on your council tax. (This does not apply in Northern Ireland.) You may also get a reduction if someone in the property has a disability. People on a low income or who receive benefits such as Income Support or Jobseeker's Allowance can get Council Tax Benefit. You can get advice on this from the local authority or the Citizens Advice Bureau.

BUILDINGS AND HOUSEHOLD INSURANCE

> **Mediation organisations can help neighbours to solve their disputes without having to go to court. Mediators talk to both sides and try to find a solution acceptable to both.**

If you buy a home with a mortgage, you must insure the building against fire, theft and accidental damage. The landlord should arrange insurance for rented buildings. It is also wise to insure your possessions against theft or damage. There are many companies that provide insurance.

NEIGHBOURS

If you live in rented accommodation, you will have a tenancy agreement. This explains all the conditions of your tenancy. It will probably include information on what to do if you have problems with your housing. Occasionally, there may be problems with your neighbours. If you do have problems with your neighbours, they can usually be solved by speaking to them first. If you cannot solve the problem, speak to your landlord, local authority or housing association. Keep a record of the problems in case you have to show exactly what the problems are and when they started. Neighbours who cause a very serious nuisance may be taken to court and can be evicted from their home.

There are several mediation organisations which help neighbours to solve their disputes without having to go to court. Mediators talk to both sides and try to find a solution acceptable to both. You can get details of mediation organisations from the local authority, Citizens Advice, and Mediation UK on 0117 904 6661 or visit: www.mediationuk.co.uk

Check that you understand:

- the process for buying and renting accommodation
- where to get advice about accommodation and moving
- the role of the estate agent
- housing priorities for local authorities
- where to get help if you are homeless
- how you can pay for the gas, water and electricity you use at home
- recycling your waste
- what council tax pays for, and
- what to do if you have problems with your neighbours.

Money and credit

Bank notes in the UK come in denominations (values) of £5, £10, £20 and £50. Northern Ireland and Scotland have their own bank notes which are valid everywhere in the UK, though sometimes people may not realise this and may not wish to accept them.

THE EURO

In January 2002 twelve European Union (EU) states adopted the euro as their common currency. The UK Government decided not to adopt the euro at that time, and has said it will only do so if the British people vote for the euro in a referendum. The euro does circulate to some extent in Northern Ireland, particularly in the towns near the border with Ireland.

> **"** To open a bank account, you need to show documents to prove your identity, such as a passport, immigration document or driving licence. **"**

FOREIGN CURRENCY

You can get or change foreign currency at banks, building societies, large post offices and exchange shops or bureaux de change. You might have to order some currencies in advance. The exchange rates vary and you should check for the best deal.

BANKS AND BUILDING SOCIETIES

Most adults in the UK have a bank or building society account. Many large national banks or building societies have branches in towns and cities throughout the UK. It is worth checking the different types of account each one offers. Many employers pay salaries directly into a bank or building society account. There are many banks and building societies to choose from. To open an account, you need to show documents to prove your identity, such as a passport, immigration document or driving licence. You also need to show something with your address on it like a tenancy agreement or household bill. It is also possible to open bank accounts in some supermarkets or on the internet.

CASH AND DEBIT CARDS

Cash cards allow you to use cash machines to withdraw money from your account. For this you need a Personal Identification Number (PIN) which you must keep secret. A debit card allows you to pay for things without using cash. You must have enough money in your account to cover what you buy. If you lose your cash card or debit card you must inform the bank immediately.

CREDIT AND STORE CARDS

Credit cards can be used to buy things in shops, on the telephone and over the internet. A store card is like a credit card but used only in a specific shop. Credit and store cards do not draw money from your bank account, but you will be sent a bill every month. If you do not pay the total amount on the bill, you are charged interest. Although credit and store cards are useful, the interest is usually very high and many people fall into debt this way. If you lose your credit or store cards you must inform the company immediately.

CREDIT AND LOANS

People in the UK often borrow money from banks and other organisations to pay for things like household goods, cars and holidays. This is more common in the UK than in many other countries. You must be very sure of the terms and conditions when you decide to take out a loan. You can get advice on loans from the Citizens Advice Bureau if you are uncertain.

BEING REFUSED CREDIT

Banks and other organisations use different information about you to make a decision about a loan, such as your occupation, address, salary and previous credit record. If you apply for a loan you might be refused. If this happens, you have the right to ask the reason why.

CREDIT UNIONS

Credit unions are financial co-operatives owned and controlled by their members. The members pool their savings and then make loans from this pool. Interest rates in credit unions are usually lower than banks and building societies. There are credit unions in many cities and towns. To find the nearest credit union contact the Association of British Credit Unions (ABCUL) on: www.abcul.coop

INSURANCE

As well as insuring their property and possessions (see above), many people insure their credit cards and mobile phones. They

> **Although credit and store cards are useful, the interest is usually very high and many people fall into debt this way.**

also buy insurance when they travel abroad in case they lose their luggage or need medical treatment. Insurance is compulsory if you have a car or motorcycle. You can usually arrange insurance directly with an insurance company, or you can use a broker who will help you get the best deal.

> "Guides to benefits are available from Jobcentre Plus offices, local libraries, post offices and the Citizens Advice Bureau"

SOCIAL SECURITY

The UK has a system of social security which pays welfare benefits to people who do not have enough money to live on. Benefits are usually available for the sick and disabled, older people, the unemployed and those on low incomes. People who do not have legal rights of residence (or 'settlement') in the UK cannot usually receive benefits. Arrangements for paying and receiving benefits are complex because they have to cover people in many different situations. Guides to benefits are available from Jobcentre Plus offices, local libraries, post offices and the Citizens Advice Bureau.

✓ **Check that you understand:**

- what you need to open a bank account or building society account
- what debit, credit and store cards are
- what a credit union is
- what insurance is, and
- how to get help with benefits and problems with debt.

Health

Healthcare in the UK is organised under the National Health Service (NHS). The NHS began in 1948, and is one of the largest organisations in Europe. It provides all residents with free healthcare and treatment.

FINDING A DOCTOR

Family doctors are called General Practitioners (GPs) and they work in surgeries. GPs often work together in a group practice. This is sometimes called a Primary Health Care Centre.

Your GP is responsible for organising the health treatment you receive. Treatment can be for physical and mental illnesses. If you need to see a specialist, you must go to your GP first. Your GP will then refer you to a specialist in a hospital. Your GP can also refer you for specialist treatment if you have special needs.

You can get a list of local GPs from libraries, post offices, the tourist information office, the Citizens Advice Bureau, the local health authority and from the following websites:

- www.nhs.uk for health practitioners in England

- www.wales.nhs.uk/directory.cfm for health practitioners in Wales

- www.n-i.nhs.uk for health practitioners in Northern Ireland, and

- www.show.scot.nhs.uk/findnearest/healthservices in Scotland.

You can also ask neighbours and friends for the name of their local doctor.

You can attend a hospital without a GP's letter only in the case of an emergency. If you have an emergency you should go to the Accident and Emergency (A & E) department of the nearest hospital.

> " You should look for a GP as soon as you move to a new area. You should not wait until you are ill. "

REGISTERING WITH A GP

You should look for a GP as soon as you move to a new area. You should not wait until you are ill. The health centre, or surgery, will tell you what you need to do to register. Usually you must have a medical card. If you do not have one, the GP's receptionist should give you a form to send to the local health authority. They will then send you a medical card.

Before you register you should check the surgery can offer what you need. For example, you might need a woman GP, or maternity services. Sometimes GPs have many patients and are unable to accept new ones. If you cannot find a GP, you can ask your local health authority to help you find one.

USING YOUR DOCTOR

> **In exceptional circumstances, GPs can visit patients at home but they always give priority to people who are unable to travel.**

All patients registering with a GP are entitled to a free health check. Appointments to see the GP can be made by phone or in person. Sometimes you might have to wait several days before you can see a doctor. If you need immediate medical attention, ask for an urgent appointment. You should go to the GP's surgery a few minutes before the appointment. If you cannot attend or do not need the appointment any more, you must let the surgery know. The GP needs patients to answer all questions as fully as possible in order to find out what is wrong. Everything you tell the GP is completely confidential and cannot be passed on to anyone else without your permission. If you do not understand something, ask for clarification. If you have difficulties with English, bring someone who can help you, or ask the receptionist for an interpreter. This must be done when you make the appointment. If you have asked for an interpreter, it is important that you keep your appointment because this service is expensive.

In exceptional circumstances, GPs can visit patients at home but they always give priority to people who are unable to travel. If you call the GP outside normal working hours, you will have to answer several questions about your situation. This is to assess how serious your case is. You will then be told if a doctor can come to your home. You might be advised to go to the nearest A & E department.

CHARGES

Prescription charges were scrapped in Wales in 2007, Northern Ireland in 2010 and will be abolished in Scotland in 2011. However, for the purposes of your test you must learn the text as reproduced here.

Treatment from the GP is free but you have to pay a charge for your medicines and for certain services, such as vaccinations for travel abroad. If the GP decides you need to take medicine you will be given a prescription. You must take this to a pharmacy (chemist).

PRESCRIPTIONS

Prescriptions are free for anyone who is:

- under 16 years of age (under 25 in Wales)
- under 19 and in full-time education

- aged 60 or over

- pregnant or with a baby under 12 months old

- suffering from a specified medical condition, or

- receiving Income Support, Jobseeker's Allowance, Working Families or Disabilities Tax Credit.

FEELING UNWELL

If you or your child feels unwell you have the following options:

For information or advice

- ask your local pharmacist (chemist). The pharmacy can give advice on medicines and some illnesses and conditions that are not serious

- speak to a nurse by phoning NHS Direct on 0845 46 47, or

- use the NHS Direct website, NHS Direct Online: www.nhsdirect.nhs.uk

To see a doctor or nurse

- make an appointment to see your GP or a nurse working in the surgery

- visit an NHS walk-in centre.

For urgent medical treatment

- contact your GP

- go to your nearest hospital with an Accident and Emergency department, or

- call 999 for an ambulance. Calls are free. ONLY use this service for a real emergency.

A pharmacy can give advice on medicines and some illnesses and conditions that are not serious.

NHS Direct is a 24-hour telephone service which provides information on particular health conditions. Telephone: 0845 46 47. You may ask for an interpreter for advice in your own language. In Scotland, find NHS24 at: www.nhs24.com or telephone: 08454 24 24 24.

NHS Direct Online is a website providing information about health services and several medical conditions and treatments: www.nhsdirect.nhs.uk

NHS walk-in centres provide treatment for minor injuries and

Dental examinations are free in Scotland. Note this does not include treatment, although certain groups are eligible for free treatment. For details please see www.lifeintheuk.net. However, for the purposes of your test you must learn the text as reproduced here.

illnesses seven days a week. You do not need an appointment. For details of your nearest centre call NHS Direct or visit the NHS website at: www.nhs.uk (for Northern Ireland www.n-i.nhs.uk) and click on 'local NHS services'.

GOING INTO HOSPITAL

If you need minor tests at a hospital, you will probably attend the outpatients department. If your treatment takes several hours, you will go into hospital as a day patient. If you need to stay overnight, you will go into hospital as an inpatient.

You should take personal belongings with you, such as a towel, night clothes, things for washing, and a dressing gown. You will receive all your meals while you are an inpatient. If you need advice about going into hospital, contact Customer Services or the Patient Advice and Liaison Service (PALS) at the hospital where you will receive treatment.

DENTISTS

You can get the name of a dentist by asking at the local library, at the Citizens Advice Bureau and through NHS Direct. Most people have to pay for dental treatment. Some dentists work for the NHS and some are private. NHS dentists charge less than private dentists, but some dentists have two sets of charges, both NHS and private. A dentist should explain your treatment and the charges before the treatment begins.

Free dental treatment is available to:

- people under 18 (in Wales people under 25 and over 60)

- pregnant women and women with babies under 12 months old, and

- people on Income Support, Jobseeker's Allowance or Pension Credit Guarantee.

OPTICIANS

Most people have to pay for sight tests and glasses, except children, people over 60, people with certain eye conditions and people receiving certain benefits. In Scotland, eye tests are free.

PREGNANCY AND CARE OF YOUNG CHILDREN

If you are pregnant you will receive regular antenatal care. This is available from your local hospital, local health centre or from special antenatal clinics. You will receive support from a GP and from a midwife. Midwives work in hospitals or health centres. Some GPs do not provide maternity services so you may wish to look for another GP during your pregnancy. In the UK women usually have their babies in hospital, especially if it is their first baby. It is common for the father to attend the birth, but only if the mother wants him to be there.

A short time after you have your child, you will begin regular contact with a health visitor. She or he is a qualified nurse and can advise you about caring for your baby. The first visits will be in your home, but after that you might meet the health visitor at a clinic. You can ask advice from your health visitor until your child is five years old. In most towns and cities there are mother and toddler groups or playgroups for small children. These often take place at local churches and community centres. You might be able to send your child to a nursery school (see **Going to school**).

> " You can ask advice from your health visitor until your child is five years old. "

Information on pregnancy

You can get information on maternity and antenatal services in your area from your local health authority, a health visitor or your GP. The number of your health authority will be in the phone book.

The Family Planning Association (FPA) gives advice on contraception and sexual health. The FPA's helpline is 0845 310 1334, or: www.fpa.org.uk

The National Childbirth Trust gives information and support in pregnancy, childbirth and early parenthood: www.nctpregnancyandbabycare.com

REGISTERING A BIRTH

You must register your baby with the Registrar of Births, Marriages and Deaths (Register Office) within six weeks of the birth. The address of your local Register Office is in the phone book. If the parents are married, either the mother or father can register the birth. If they are not married, only the mother can register the birth. If the parents are not married but want both names on the child's birth certificate, both mother and father must be present when they register their baby.

In Scotland you must register your baby within 21 days of the birth. However, for the purposes of your test you must learn the text as reproduced here.

Check that you understand:

- how to find and register with a GP

- what to do if you feel unwell

- how to find other services such as dentists and opticians

- when it is possible to attend A & E without a doctor's letter

- who can get free prescriptions

- when you should phone 999 or 112

- what NHS Direct can do

- who can give health advice and treatment when you are pregnant and after you have a baby, and

- how to register a birth.

Education

GOING TO SCHOOL

Education in the UK is free and compulsory for all children between the ages of 5 and 16 (4 to 16 in Northern Ireland). The education system varies in England, Scotland, Wales and Northern Ireland.

The child's parent or guardian is responsible for making sure their child goes to school, arrives on time and attends for the whole school year. If they do not do this, the parent or guardian may be prosecuted.

Some areas of the country offer free nursery education for children over the age of 3. In most parts of the UK, compulsory education is divided into two stages, primary and secondary. In some places there is a middle-school system. In England and Wales the primary stage lasts from 5 to 11, in Scotland from 5 to 12 and in Northern Ireland from 4 to 11. The secondary stage lasts until the age of 16. At that age young people can choose to leave school or to continue with their education until they are 17 or 18.

Details of local schools are available from your local education authority office or website. The addresses and phone numbers of local education authorities are in the phone book.

> For children starting secondary school in or after 2008 the leaving age will be 17, for those starting in or after 2009 the leaving age will be 18. For details on these please see www.lifeintheuk.net. However, for the purposes of your test you must learn the text as reproduced here. See also p105.

PRIMARY SCHOOLS

These are usually schools where both boys and girls learn together and are usually close to a child's home. Children tend to be with the same group and teacher all day. Schools encourage parents to help their children with learning, particularly with reading and writing.

SECONDARY SCHOOLS

At age 11 (12 in Scotland) children go to secondary school. This might normally be the school nearest their home, but parents in England and Wales are allowed to express a preference for a different school. In some areas, getting a secondary school place in a preferred school can be difficult, and parents often apply to several schools in order to make sure their child gets offered a place. In Northern Ireland many schools select children through a test taken at the age of 11.

If the preferred school has enough places, the child will be offered a place. If there are not enough places, children will be offered places according to the school's admission arrangements. Admission arrangements vary from area to area.

Secondary schools are larger than primary schools. Most are mixed sex, although there are single-sex schools in some areas. Your local education authority will give you information on schools in your area. It will also tell you which schools have spaces and give you information about why some children will be given places when only a few are available and why other children might not. It will also tell you how to apply for a secondary school place.

COSTS

Education at state schools in the UK is free, but parents have to pay for school uniforms and sports wear. There are sometimes extra charges for music lessons and for school outings. Parents on low incomes can get help with costs, and with the cost of school meals. You can get advice on this from the local education authority or the Citizens Advice Bureau.

CHURCH AND OTHER FAITH SCHOOLS

Some primary and secondary schools in the UK are linked to the Church of England or the Roman Catholic Church. These are called 'faith schools'. In some areas there are Muslim, Jewish and Sikh schools. In Northern Ireland, some schools are called Integrated Schools. These schools aim to bring children of different religions together. Information on faith schools is available from your local education authority.

INDEPENDENT SCHOOLS

Independent schools are private schools. They are not run or paid for by the state. Independent secondary schools are also sometimes called public schools. There are about 2,500 independent schools in the UK. About 8% of children go to these schools. At independent schools parents must pay the full cost of their child's education. Some independent schools offer scholarships which pay some or all of the costs of the child's education.

THE SCHOOL CURRICULUM

All state, primary and secondary schools in England, Wales and Northern Ireland follow the National Curriculum. This covers

> Education at state schools in the UK is free, but parents have to pay for school uniforms and sports wear. There are sometimes extra charges for music lessons and for school outings.

There are now around 2,300 independent schools in the UK and around 7% of children go to these schools. However, for the purposes of your test you must learn the text as reproduced here.

English, maths, science, design and technology, information and communication technology (ICT), history, geography, modern foreign languages, art and design, music, physical education (PE) and citizenship. In Wales, children learn Welsh.

In some primary schools in Wales, all the lessons are taught in Welsh. In Scotland, pupils follow a broad curriculum informed by national guidance. Schools must, by law, provide religious education (RE) to all pupils. Parents are allowed to withdraw their children from these lessons. RE lessons have a Christian basis but children also learn about the other major religions.

ASSESSMENT

In England, the curriculum is divided into four stages, called Key Stages. After each stage children are tested. They take Key Stage tests (also called SATs) at ages 7, 11 and 14. At 16 they usually take the General Certificates of Secondary Education (GCSEs) in several subjects, although some schools also offer other qualifications. At 18, young people who have stayed at school do AGCEs (Advanced GCE levels) often just called A-levels.

In Wales, schools follow the Welsh National Curriculum but have abolished national tests for children at age 7 and 11. There are also plans in Wales to stop testing children at 14. Teachers in Wales still have to assess and report on their pupils' progress and achievements at 7 and 11.

In Scotland, the curriculum is divided into two phases. The first phase is from 5 to 14. There are six levels in this phase, levels A to F. There are no tests for whole groups during this time. Teachers test individual children when they are ready. From 14 to 16, young people do Standard Grade. After 16 they can study at Intermediate, Higher or Advanced level. In Scotland there will soon be a single curriculum for all pupils from age 3 to age 18. This is called 'A Curriculum for Excellence'. More information can be found at: www.acurriculumforexcellencescotland.gov.uk

HELP WITH ENGLISH

If your child's main language is not English, the school may arrange for extra language support from an EAL (English Additional Language) specialist teacher.

> " In England, children usually take the General Certificates of Secondary Education (GCSEs) when they are 16. "

Since 2008 there have been many changes in the national curriculums of England, Scotland and Wales. For details on these please see www. lifeintheuk.net. For the purposes of your test you must learn the text as reproduced here. See also p33.

CAREERS EDUCATION

All children get careers advice from the age of 14. Advice is also available from Connexions, a national service for young people. Telephone: 080 800 13 2 19 or: www.connexions-direct.com in England. In Wales, Careers Wales offers advice to children from the age of 11. For further information visit: www.careerswales.com or telephone: 0800 100 900.

In Scotland, Careers Scotland provides information, services and support to all ages and stages. For further information visit: www.careers-scotland.org.uk or telephone: 0845 8 502 502.

PARENTS AND SCHOOLS

> **Schools must be open 190 days a year. Term dates are decided by the governing body or by the local education authority.**

Many parents are involved with their child's school. A number of places on a school's governing body are reserved for parents. The governing body decides how the school is run and administered and produces reports on the progress of the school from year to year. In Scotland, parents can be members of school boards or parent councils.

Schools must be open 190 days a year. Term dates are decided by the governing body or by the local education authority. Children must attend the whole school year. Schools expect parents and guardians to inform them if their child is going to be absent from school. All schools ask parents to sign a home-school agreement. This is a list of things that both the school and the parent or guardian agree to do to ensure a good education for the child. All parents receive a report every year on their child's progress. They also have the chance to go to the school to talk to their child's teachers.

FURTHER EDUCATION AND ADULT EDUCATION

> **The EMA was replaced by the 16 to 19 bursary on 1 January 2011. For the purposes of your test you must learn the text as reproduced here.**

At 16, young people can leave school or stay on to do A-levels (Higher Grades in Scotland) in preparation for university. Some young people go to their local further education (FE) college to improve their exam grades or to get new qualifications for a career. Most courses are free up to the age of 19. Young people from families with low incomes can get financial help with their studies when they leave school at 16. This is called the Education Maintenance Allowance (EMA). Information about this is available at your local college or at: www.dfes.gov.uk

Further education colleges also offer courses to adults over the age of 18. These include courses for people wishing to improve their skills in English. These courses are called ESOL (English for Speakers of Other Languages). There are also courses for English speakers who need to improve their literacy and numeracy and for people who need to learn new skills for employment. ESOL courses are also available in community centres and training centres. There is sometimes a waiting list for ESOL courses because demand is high. In England and Wales, ESOL, literacy and numeracy courses are also called Skills for Life courses. You can get information at your local college or local library or from Learndirect on 0800 100 900.

Many people join other adult education classes to learn a new skill or hobby and to meet new people. Classes are very varied and range from sports to learning a musical instrument or a new language. Details are usually available from your local library, college or adult education centre.

UNIVERSITY

More young people go to university now than in the past. Many go after A-levels (or Higher Grades in Scotland) at age 18 but it is also possible to go to university later in life. At present, most students in England, Wales and Northern Ireland have to pay towards the cost of their tuition fees and to pay for their living expenses. In Scotland there are no tuition fees but after students finish university they pay back some of the cost of their education in a payment called an endowment. At present, universities can charge up to £3,000 per year for their tuition fees, but students do not have to pay anything towards their fees before or during their studies. The government pays their tuition fees and then charges for them when a student starts working after university. Some families on low incomes receive help with their children's tuition fees. This is called a grant. The universities also give help, in the form of bursaries. Most students get a low-interest student loan from a bank. This pays for their living costs while they are at university. When a student finishes university and starts working, he or she must pay back the loan.

More young people go to university now than in the past. Many go after A-levels (or Higher Grades in Scotland) at age 18 but it is also possible to go to university later in life.

University tuition fees are capped at £3,375 for 2011/12. Fees for courses starting in 2012/13 will be capped at £9,000. For the purposes of your test you must learn the text as reproduced here.

Check that you understand:

- the different stages of a child's education

- that there are differences in the education systems in England, Scotland, Wales and Northern Ireland

- that there are different kinds of school, and that some of them charge fees

- what the National Curriculum is

- what the governing body of a school does

- options for young people at the age of 16

- courses available at FE colleges, and

- where you can get English classes or other education for adults, including university.

Leisure

INFORMATION

Information about theatre, cinema, music and exhibitions is found in local newspapers, local libraries and tourist information offices. Many museums and art galleries are free.

FILM, VIDEO AND DVD

Films in the UK have a system to show if they are suitable for children. This is called the classification system. If a child is below the age of the classification, they should not watch the film at a cinema or on DVD. All films receive a classification, as follows:

 U (Universal): Suitable for anyone aged 4 years and over

 PG (Parental Guidance): Suitable for everyone but some parts of the film might be unsuitable for children. Their parents should decide

 **12 or 12A:** Children under 12 are not allowed to see or rent the film unless they are with an adult

 15: Children under 15 are not allowed to see or rent the film

 18: No one under 18 is allowed to see or rent the film

 R18: No one under 18 is allowed to see the film, which is only available in specially licensed cinemas

TELEVISION AND RADIO

Anyone in the UK with a television (TV), DVD or video recorder, computer or any device which is used for watching or recording TV programmes must be covered by a valid television licence. One licence covers all of the equipment at one address, but people who rent different rooms in a shared house must each buy a separate licence.

A colour TV licence currently costs £131.50 (2006) and lasts for 12 months. People aged 75 or over can apply for a free TV licence. Blind people can claim a 50% discount on their TV licence. You

> A colour TV licence costs £145.50 per annum at time of publication. For the purposes of your test you must learn the text as reproduced here.

risk prosecution and a fine if you watch TV but are not covered by a TV licence. There are many ways to buy a TV licence including from local PayPoint outlets or online at: www.tvlicensing.co.uk. It is also possible to pay for the licence in instalments. For more information telephone: 0870 576 3763 or write to TV Licensing, Bristol, BS98 1TL.

SPORTS, CLUBS AND SOCIETIES

Information about local clubs and societies can usually be found at local libraries or through your local authority. For information about sports you should ask in the local leisure centre. Libraries and leisure centres often organise activities for children during the school holidays.

One TV licence covers all of the equipment at one address, but people who rent different rooms in a shared house must each buy a separate licence.

PLACES OF INTEREST

The UK has a large network of public footpaths in the countryside. Many parts of the countryside and places of interest are kept open by the National Trust. This is a charity that works to preserve important buildings and countryside in the UK. Information about National Trust buildings and areas open to the public is available on: www.nationaltrust.org.uk

PUBS AND NIGHT CLUBS

Public houses, or pubs, are an important part of social life in the UK. To drink alcohol in a pub you must be 18 or over. People under 18 are not allowed to buy alcohol in a supermarket or in an off-licence either. The landlord of the pub may allow people of 14 to come into the pub but they are not allowed to drink. At 16, people can drink wine or beer with a meal in a hotel or restaurant.

→ OVER 18

Allowed to drink alcohol in a pub

→ OVER 16

Allowed to drink wine or beer with a meal in a hotel or restaurant

→ OVER 14

May be allowed into a pub, but not allowed to drink

Pubs are usually open during the day and until 11pm. If a pub wants to stay open later, it must apply for a special licence. Night clubs open and close later than pubs.

BETTING AND GAMBLING

People under 18 are not allowed into betting shops or gambling clubs. There is a National Lottery for which draws, with large prizes, are made every week. You can enter by buying a ticket or a scratch card. People under 16 are not allowed to buy a lottery ticket or scratch card.

PETS

Many people in the UK have pets such as cats and dogs. It is against the law to treat a pet cruelly or to neglect it. All dogs in public places must wear a collar showing the name and address of the owner. The owner is responsible for keeping the dog under control and for cleaning up after the animal in a public place. Vaccinations and medical treatment for animals are available from veterinary surgeons (vets). If you cannot afford to pay a vet, you can go to a charity called the PDSA (People's Dispensary for Sick Animals). To find your nearest branch, visit: www.pdsa.org.uk

> **People under 18 are not allowed into betting shops or gambling clubs.**

Watch & Learn:

www.lifeintheuk.net/2012ec5

Scan to watch a video explaining what happens at significant ages in the UK.

Travel and transport

TRAINS, BUSES AND COACHES

Usually, tickets for trains and underground systems such as the London Underground must be bought before you get on the train. The fare varies according to the day and time you wish to travel. Travelling in the rush hour is always more expensive. Discount tickets are available for families, people aged 60 and over, disabled people, students and people under 26. Ask at your local train station for details. Failure to buy a ticket may result in a penalty.

> " Discount train tickets are available for families, people aged 60 and over, disabled people, students and people under 26. "

For information about trains telephone the National Rail Enquiry Service: 08457 48 49 50, or visit: www.nationalrail.co.uk. For trains in Northern Ireland, phone Translink on 028 90 66 66 30 or visit: www.translink.co.uk. For information about local bus times phone 0870 608 250. For information on coaches, telephone National Express on 08705 80 80 80, or visit: www.nationalexpress.com. For coaches in Scotland, telephone Scottish Citylink on 08705 50 50 50 or visit: www.citylink.co.uk. For Northern Ireland, visit: www.translink.co.uk

TAXIS

To operate legally, all taxis and minicabs must be licensed and display a licence plate. Taxis and cabs with no licence are not insured for fare-paying passengers and are not always safe. Women should not use unlicensed minicabs.

→ 17 YEARS OLD
→ 18 YEARS OLD
→ 21 YEARS OLD

to drive a car or motorcycle   to drive a medium-sized lorry   to drive a large lorry or bus

DRIVING

You must be at least 17 to drive a car or motorcycle, 18 to drive a medium-sized lorry, and 21 to drive a large lorry or bus. To drive a lorry, minibus or bus with more than eight passenger seats, you must have a special licence.

THE DRIVING LICENCE

You must have a driving licence to drive on public roads. To get a driving licence you must pass a test. There are many driving schools where you can learn with the help of a qualified instructor.

You get a full driving licence in three stages:

1. Apply for a provisional licence. You need this licence while you are learning to drive. With this you are allowed to drive a motorcycle up to 125cc or a car. You must put L plates on the vehicle, or D plates in Wales. Learner drivers cannot drive on a motorway. If you drive a car, you must be with someone who is over 21 and who has had a full licence for over three years. You can get an application form for a provisional licence from a post office.

2. Pass a written theory test.

3. Pass a practical driving test.

Drivers may use their licence until they are 70. After that the licence is valid for three years at a time.

In Northern Ireland, a newly qualified driver must display an R-plate (for registered driver) for one year after passing the test.

OVERSEAS LICENCES

If your driving licence is from a country in the European Union (EU), Iceland, Liechtenstein or Norway, you can drive in the UK for as long as your licence is valid.

If you have a licence from a country outside the EU, you may use it in the UK for up to 12 months. During this time you must get a UK provisional driving licence and pass both the UK theory and practical driving tests, or you will not be able to drive after 12 months.

INSURANCE

It is a criminal offence to have a car without proper motor insurance. Drivers without insurance can receive very high fines. It is also illegal to allow someone to use your car if they are not insured to drive it.

> " You must be at least 17 to drive a car or motorcycle, 18 to drive a medium-sized lorry, and 21 to drive a large lorry or bus. "

ROAD TAX AND MOT

You must also pay a tax to drive your car on the roads. This is called road tax. Your vehicle must have a road tax disc which shows you have paid. You can buy this at the post office. If you do not pay the road tax, your vehicle may be clamped or towed away.

If your vehicle is over three years old, you must take it every year for a Ministry of Transport (MOT) test. You can do this at an approved garage. The garage will give you an MOT certificate when your car passes the test. It is an offence not to have an MOT certificate. If you do not have an MOT certificate, your insurance will not be valid.

SAFETY

> "
> If your vehicle is over three years old, you must take it every year for a Ministry of Transport (MOT) test. You can do this at an approved garage.
> "

Everyone in a vehicle should wear a seat belt. Children under 12 years of age may need a special booster seat. Motorcyclists and their passengers must wear a crash helmet (this law does not apply to Sikh men if they are wearing a turban). It is illegal to drive while holding a mobile phone.

SPEED LIMITS

For cars and motorcycles the speed limits are:

- 30 miles per hour (mph) in built-up areas, unless a sign shows a different limit
- 60 mph on single carriageways
- 70 mph on motorways and dual carriageways

30 mph
in built-up areas

60 mph
on single carriageways

70 mph
on motorways
or dual carriageways

Speed limits are lower for buses, lorries and cars pulling caravans.

It is illegal to drive when you are over the alcohol limit or drunk. The police can stop you and give you a test to see how much alcohol you have in your body. This is called a breathalyser test. If a driver has more than the permitted amount of alcohol (called being 'over the limit') or refuses to take the test, he or she will be arrested. People who drink and drive can expect to be disqualified from driving for a long period.

ACCIDENTS

If you are involved in a road accident:

- don't drive away without stopping – this is a criminal offence
- call the police and ambulance on 999 or 112 if someone is injured
- get the names, addresses, vehicle registration numbers and insurance details of the other drivers
- give your details to the other drivers or passengers and to the police, and
- make a note of everything that happened and contact your insurance company as soon as possible.

Note that if you admit the accident was your fault, the insurance company may refuse to pay. It is better to wait until the insurance company decides for itself whose fault the accident was.

66

It is illegal to drive when you are over the alcohol limit or drunk. The police can stop you and give you a test to see how much alcohol you have in your body. This is called a breathalyser test.

99

Identity documents

At present, UK citizens do not have to carry identity (ID) cards. The government is, however, making plans to introduce them in the next few years.

PROVING YOUR IDENTITY

You may have to prove your identity at different times, such as when you open a bank account, rent accommodation, enrol for a college course, hire a car, apply for benefits such as Housing Benefit or apply for a marriage certificate. Different organisations may ask for different documents as proof of identity. These can include:

- official documents from the Home Office showing your immigration status
- a certificate of identity
- a passport or travel document
- a National Insurance (NI) number card
- a provisional or full driving licence
- a recent gas, electricity or phone bill showing your name and address, or
- a rent or benefits book.

✓ **Check that you understand:**

- how films are classified
- why you need a television licence
- the rules about the selling and drinking of alcohol
- how to get a driving licence
- what you need to do to be allowed to drive a vehicle in the UK
- what you should do if you have an accident, and
- when you might have to prove your identity, and how you can do it.

CHAPTER 6
Employment

→ **IN THIS CHAPTER** you will learn about working in Britain. Much of what you need to learn relates to your rights and responsibilities as an employee. As an employee, you should always be treated fairly in terms of pay, health and safety and access to opportunities. At the same time, you must also behave honestly and meet your obligations such as tax and National Insurance. You also have to understand the rules and rights for families in relation to employment. This includes both the rights that parents have to spend time with their children but also the strict limitations that are in place to ensure that children are not exploited in the workplace, so that they are able to pursue their education without interference.

IN THIS CHAPTER THERE IS INFORMATION ABOUT:
- Looking for work and applying for jobs
- Training and volunteering
- Equal rights and discrimination
- Rights and responsibilities at work
- Working for yourself
- Childcare and children at work

Looking for work

If you are looking for work, or you are thinking of changing your job, there are a number of ways you can find out about work opportunities. The Home Office provides guidance on who is allowed to work in the UK. Not everyone in the UK is allowed to work and some people need work permits, so it is important to check your status before taking up work. Also, employers have to check that anyone they employ is legally entitled to work in the UK. For more information and guidance, see the Home Office website 'Working in the UK' at www.workingintheuk.gov.uk

Jobs are usually advertised in local and national newspapers, at the local Jobcentre and in employment agencies. You can find the address and telephone number of your local Jobcentre under Jobcentre Plus in the phone book or see: www.jobcentreplus.gov.uk. Some jobs are advertised on supermarket notice boards and in shop windows. These jobs are usually part-time and the wages are often quite low. If there are particular companies you would like to work for, you can look for vacancies on their websites.

Jobcentre Plus is run by a government department – the Department for Work and Pensions. Trained staff give advice and help in finding and applying for jobs as well as claiming benefits. They can also arrange for interpreters. Their website, www.jobcentreplus.gov.uk, lists vacancies and training opportunities and gives general information on benefits. There is also a low-cost telephone service – Jobseeker Direct, 0845 60 60 234. This is open 9am to 6pm on weekdays and 9am to 1pm on Saturdays.

> **"** If you have qualifications from another country, you can find out how they compare with qualifications in the UK at the National Academic Recognition Information Centre (NARIC). **"**

QUALIFICATIONS

Applicants for some jobs need special training or qualifications. If you have qualifications from another country, you can find out how they compare with qualifications in the UK at the National Academic Recognition Information Centre (NARIC), www.naric.org.uk

For further information contact UK NARIC, ECCTIS Ltd, Oriel House, Oriel Road, Cheltenham, Glos, GL50 1XP, telephone: 0870 990 4088, email: info@naric.org.uk

APPLICATIONS

Interviews for lower-paid and local jobs can often be arranged by telephone or in person. For many jobs you need to fill in an application form or send a copy of your curriculum vitae (CV) with a covering letter or letter of application.

A covering letter is usually a short letter attached to a completed application form, while a letter of application gives more detailed information on why you are applying for the job and why you think you are suitable. Your CV gives specific details on your education, qualifications, previous employment, skills and interests. It is important to type any letters and your CV on a computer or word processor as this improves your chance of being called for an interview.

Employers often ask for the names and addresses of one or two referees. These are people such as your current or previous employer or college tutor. Referees need to know you well and to agree to write a short report or reference on your suitability for the job. Personal friends or members of your family are not normally acceptable as referees.

INTERVIEWS

In job descriptions and interviews, employers should give full details of what the job involves, including the pay, holidays and working conditions. If you need more information about any of these, you can ask questions in the interview. In fact, asking some questions in the interview shows you are interested and can improve your chance of getting the job.

When you are applying for a job and during the interview, it is important to be honest about your qualifications and experience. If an employer later finds out that you gave incorrect information, you might lose your job.

CRIMINAL RECORD

For some jobs, particularly if the work involves working with children or vulnerable people, the employer will ask for your permission to do a criminal record check. You can get more information on this from the Home Office Criminal Records Bureau (CRB) information line, telephone: 0870 90 90 811. In Scotland, contact Disclosure Scotland: www.disclosurescotland.co.uk, helpline: 0870 609 6006.

A covering letter is usually a short letter attached to a completed application form, while a letter of application gives more detailed information on why you are applying for the job and why you think you are suitable.

TRAINING

Taking up training helps people improve their qualifications for work. Some training may be offered at work or you can do courses from home or at your local college. This includes English language training. You can get more information from your local library and college or from websites such as www.worktrain.gov.uk and www.learndirect.co.uk. Learndirect offers a range of online training courses at centres across the country. There are charges for courses but you can do free starter or taster sessions. You can get more information from their free information and advice line: telephone 0800 100 900.

VOLUNTEERING AND WORK EXPERIENCE

Some people do voluntary work and this can be a good way to support your local community and organisations which depend on volunteers. It also provides useful experience that can help with future job applications. Your local library will have information about volunteering opportunities.

You can also get information and advice from websites such as: www.do-it.org.uk, www.volunteering.org.uk and www.justdo-something.net

Check that you understand:

- the Home Office provides guidance on who is entitled to work in the UK
- NARIC can advise on how qualifications from overseas compare with qualifications from the UK
- what CVs are
- who can be a referee
- what happens if any of the information you have given is untrue
- when you need a CRB check
- where you can find out about training opportunities and job seeking, and
- the benefits of volunteering in terms of work experience and community involvement.

Equal rights and discrimination

It is against the law for employers to discriminate against someone at work. This means that a person should not be refused work, training or promotion, or treated less favourably because of their:

• sex

• nationality, race, colour or ethnic group

• disability

• religion

• sexual orientation, or

• age.

In Northern Ireland, the law also bans discrimination on grounds of religious belief or political opinion.

The law also says that men and women who do the same job, or work of equal value, should receive equal pay. Almost all the laws protecting people at work apply equally to people doing part-time or full-time jobs.

There are, however, a small number of jobs where discrimination laws do not apply. For example, discrimination is not against the law when the job involves working for someone in their own home.

You can get more information about the law and racial discrimination from the Commission for Racial Equality. The Equal Opportunities Commission can help with sex discrimination issues and the Disability Rights Commission deals with disability issues. Each of these organisations offers advice and information and can, in some cases, support individuals. From October 2007 their functions will be brought together in a new Commission for Equality and Human Rights. You can get more information about the laws protecting people at work from the Citizens Advice Bureau website: www.adviceguide.org.uk

In Northern Ireland, the Equality Commission provides information and advice in respect of all forms of unlawful discrimination.

The Commission for Racial Equality, St Dunstan's House, 201–211 Borough High Street, London, SE1 1GZ
Tel: 020 7939 000, Fax: 020 7939 0001, www.cre.gov.uk

The Equality and Human Rights Commission is now in place, taking on responsibility for all aspects of equality such as race, age, sexual orientation and religion, as well as human rights. For details on these please see www.lifeintheuk.net. For the purposes of your test you must learn the text as reproduced here.

The Equal Opportunities Commission, Arndale House, Arndale Centre, Manchester M4 3EQ Tel: 0845 601 5901, Fax: 0161 838 8312, www.eoc.org.uk

The Disability Rights Commission, DRC Helpline, FREEPOST MID02164, Stratford upon Avon, CV37 9BR Tel: 08457 622 633, Fax: 08457 778 878, www.drc.org.uk

66

Men and women can be victims of sexual harassment at work. If this happens to you, tell a friend, colleague or trade union representative and ask the person harassing you to stop.

99

The Equality Commission for Northern Ireland, Equality House, 7–9 Shaftesbury Square, Belfast BT2 7DP Tel: 028 90 500 600, www.equalityni.org

SEXUAL HARASSMENT

Sexual harassment can take different forms. This includes:

• indecent remarks

• comments about the way you look that make you feel uncomfortable or humiliated

• comments or questions about your sex life

• inappropriate touching or sexual demands, and

• bullying behaviour or being treated in a way that is rude, hostile, degrading or humiliating because of your sex.

Men and women can be victims of sexual harassment at work. If this happens to you, tell a friend, colleague or trade union representative and ask the person harassing you to stop. It is a good idea to keep a written record of what happened, the days and times when it happened and who else may have seen or heard the harassment. If the problem continues, report the person to your employer or trade union. Employers are responsible for the behaviour of their employees while they are at work. They should treat complaints of sexual harassment very seriously and take effective action to deal with the problem. If you are not satisfied with your employer's response, you can ask for advice and support from the Equal Opportunities Commission, your trade union or the Citizens Advice Bureau.

At work

Both employers and employees have legal responsibilities at work. Employers have to pay employees for the work that they do, treat them fairly and take responsible care for their health and safety. Employees should do their work with reasonable skill and care and follow all reasonable instructions. They should not damage their employer's business.

A WRITTEN CONTRACT OR STATEMENT

Within two months of starting a new job, your employer should give you a written contract or statement with all the details and conditions for your work. This should include your responsibilities, pay, working hours, holidays, sick pay and pension. It should also include the period of notice that both you and your employer should give for the employment to end. The contract or written statement is an important document and is very useful if there is ever a disagreement about your work, pay or conditions.

PAY, HOURS AND HOLIDAYS

Your pay is agreed between you and your employer. There is a minimum wage in the UK that is a legal right for every employed person above compulsory school-leaving age. The compulsory school-leaving age is 16, but the time in the school year when 16-year-olds can leave school in England and Wales is different from that in Scotland and Northern Ireland.

> ❶
> The school leaving age will rise to 17 in 2014, and 18 in 2015. For details on these please see www.lifeintheuk.net. However, for the purposes of your test you must learn the text as reproduced here. See also p85.

Minimum wage rates

➜ 16–17 YEARS OLD	➜ 18–21 YEARS OLD	➜ 22 AND ABOVE
£3.30 an hour	**£4.45** an hour	**£5.35** an hour

As of October 2006

The national minimum wage rates are reviewed annually. For the latest minimum wages please see www.lifeintheuk.net. For the purposes of your test you must learn the text as reproduced here.

Employees are now entitled to 5.6 weeks' paid holiday every year. For the purposes of your test you must learn the text as reproduced here.

There are different minimum wage rates for different age groups. From October 2006 the rates are as follows:

- for workers aged 22 and above – £5.35 an hour
- for 18–21 years old – £4.45 an hour, and
- for 16–17 years old – £3.30 an hour.

Employers who pay their workers less than this are breaking the law. You can get more information from the Central Office of Information Directgov website, www.direct.gov.uk, which has a wide range of public service information. Alternatively, you can telephone the National Minimum Wage Helpline, telephone: 0845 600 0678.

Your contract or statement will show the number of hours you are expected to work. Your employer might ask you if you can work more hours than this and it is your decision whether or not you do. Your employer cannot require you to work more hours than the hours agreed on your contract.

If you need to be absent from work, for example if you are ill or you have a medical appointment, it is important to tell your employer as soon as you can in advance. Most employees who are 16 or over are entitled to at least four weeks' paid holiday every year. This includes time for national holidays (see **Chapter 3**). Your employer must give you a pay slip, or a similar written statement, each time you are paid. This must show exactly how much money has been taken off for tax and National Insurance contributions.

TAX

For most people, tax is automatically taken from their earnings by the employer and paid directly to HM Revenue & Customs, the government department responsible for collecting taxes. If you are self-employed, you need to pay your own tax (see **Working for yourself**). Money raised from income tax pays for government services such as roads, education, police and the armed forces. Occasionally HM Revenue & Customs sends out tax return forms which ask for full financial details. If you receive one, it is important to complete it and return the form as soon as possible. You can get help and advice from the HM Revenue & Customs self-assessment helpline, on: 0845 300 45 55.

NATIONAL INSURANCE

Almost everybody in the UK who is in paid work, including self-employed people, must pay National Insurance (NI) contributions. Money raised from NI contributions is used to pay contributory benefits such as the state retirement pension and helps fund the National Health Service. Employees have their NI contributions deducted from their pay by their employer every week or month. People who are self-employed need to pay NI contributions themselves: Class 2 contributions, either by direct debit or every three months, and Class 4 contributions on the profits from their trade or business. Class 4 contributions are paid alongside their income tax. Anyone who does not pay enough NI contributions will not be able to receive certain benefits, such as Jobseeker's Allowance or Maternity Pay, and may not receive a full state retirement pension.

Getting a National Insurance number

Just before their 16th birthday, all young people in the UK are sent a National Insurance number. This is a unique number for each person and it tracks their National Insurance contributions.

Refugees whose asylum applications have been successful have the same rights to work as any other UK citizen and to receive a National Insurance number. People who have applied for asylum and have not received a positive decision do not usually have permission to work and so do not get a National Insurance number.

You need a National Insurance number when you start work. If you do not have a National Insurance number, you can apply for one through Jobcentre Plus or your local Social Security Office. It is a good idea to make an appointment by telephone and ask which documents you need to take with you. You usually need to show your birth certificate, passport and Home Office documents allowing you to stay in the country. If you need information about registering for a National Insurance number, you can telephone the National Insurance Registrations Helpline on 0845 91 57006 or 0845 91 55670.

> **66**
> Anyone who does not pay enough NI contributions will not be able to receive certain benefits, such as Jobseeker's Allowance or Maternity Pay, and may not receive a full state retirement pension.
> **99**

PENSIONS

Everyone in the UK who has paid enough National Insurance contributions will get a State Pension when they retire. The State Pension age for men is currently 65 years of age and for women it is 60, but the State Pension age for women will increase to 65 in stages between 2010 and 2020. You can find full details of the State Pension scheme on the State Pension website, www.thepensionservice.gov.uk, or you can phone the Pension Service Helpline: 0845 60 60 265.

In addition to a State Pension, many people also receive a pension through their work and some also pay into a personal pension plan too. It is very important to get good advice about pensions. The Pensions Advisory Service gives free and confidential advice on occupational and personal pensions. Their helpline telephone number is 0845 601 2923 and their website address is www.opas.org.uk. Independent financial advisers can also give advice but you usually have to pay a fee for this service. You can find local financial advisers in the Yellow Pages and Thomson local guides or on the internet at www.unbiased.co.uk

> **"** The State Pension age for men is currently 65 years of age and for women it is 60, but the State Pension age for women will increase to 65 in stages between 2010 and 2020. **"**

HEALTH AND SAFETY

Employers have a legal duty to make sure the workplace is safe. Employees also have a legal duty to follow safety regulations and to work safely and responsibly. If you are worried about health and safety at your workplace, talk to your supervisor, manager or trade union representative. You need to follow the right procedures and your employer must not dismiss you or treat you unfairly for raising a concern.

TRADE UNIONS

Trade unions are organisations that aim to improve the pay and working conditions of their members. They also give their members advice and support on problems at work. You can choose whether to join a trade union or not and your employer cannot dismiss you or treat you unfairly for being a union member.

You can find details of trade unions in the UK, the benefits they offer to members and useful information on rights at work on the Trades Union Congress (TUC) website, www.tuc.org.uk

PROBLEMS AT WORK

If you have problems of any kind at work, speak to your supervisor, manager, trade union representative or someone else with responsibility as soon as possible. If you need to take any action, it is a good idea to get advice first. If you are a member of a trade union, your representative will help. You can also contact your local Citizens Advice Bureau (CAB) or Law Centre. The national

Advisory, Conciliation and Arbitration Service (ACAS) website, www.acas.org.uk, gives information on your rights at work. ACAS also offers a national helpline, telephone: 08457 47 47 47.

LOSING YOUR JOB AND UNFAIR DISMISSAL

An employee can be dismissed immediately for serious misconduct at work. Anyone who cannot do their job properly, or is unacceptably late or absent from work, should be given a warning by their employer. If their work, punctuality or attendance does not improve, the employer can give them notice to leave their job.

It is against the law for employers to dismiss someone from work unfairly. If this happens to you, or life at work is made so difficult that you feel you have to leave, you may be able to get compensation if you take your case to an Employment Tribunal. This is a court which specialises in employment matters. You normally only have three months to make a complaint.

If you are dismissed from your job, it is important to get advice on your case as soon as possible. You can ask for advice and information on your legal rights and the best action to take from your trade union representative, a solicitor, a Law Centre or the Citizens Advice Bureau.

REDUNDANCY

If you lose your job because the company you work for no longer needs someone to do your job, or cannot afford to employ you, you may be entitled to redundancy pay. The amount of money you receive depends on the length of time you have been employed. Again your trade union representative, a solicitor, a Law Centre or the Citizens Advice Bureau can advise you.

UNEMPLOYMENT

Most people who become unemployed can claim Jobseeker's Allowance (JSA). This is currently available for men aged 18–65 and women aged 18–60 who are capable of working, available for work and trying to find work. Unemployed 16- and 17-year-olds may not be eligible for Jobseeker's Allowance but may be able to claim a Young Person's Bridging Allowance (YPBA) instead. The local Jobcentre Plus can help with claims. You can get further information from the Citizens Advice Bureau and the Jobcentre Plus website: www.jobcentreplus.gov.uk

> **"**
> If you lose your job because the company you work for no longer needs someone to do your job, or cannot afford to employ you, you may be entitled to redundancy pay.
> **"**

!

The New Deal scheme has being replaced with the Flexible New Deal scheme in certain areas. For details please see www. lifeintheuk.net. However, for the purposes of your test you must learn the text as reproduced here.

NEW DEAL

New Deal is a government programme that aims to give unemployed people the help and support they need to get into work. Young people who have been unemployed for 6 months and adults who have been unemployed for 18 months are usually required to join New Deal if they wish to continue receiving a benefit. There are different New Deal schemes for different age groups. You can find out more about New Deal on 0845 606 2626 or: www.newdeal.gov.uk

The government also runs work-based learning programmes which offer training to people while they are at work. People receive a wage or an allowance and can attend college for one day a week to get a new qualification.

You can find out more about the different government schemes, and the schemes in your area, from Jobcentre Plus, www.jobcentreplus.gov.uk, or your local Citizens Advice Bureau.

Working for yourself

TAX

Self-employed people are responsible for paying their own tax and National Insurance. They have to keep detailed records of what they earn and spend on the business and send their business accounts to HM Revenue & Customs every year. Most self-employed people use an accountant to make sure they pay the correct tax and claim all the possible tax allowances.

As soon as you become self-employed you should register yourself for tax and National Insurance by ringing the HM Revenue & Customs telephone helpline for people who are self-employed, on 0845 915 4515.

HELP AND ADVICE

Banks can give information and advice on setting up your own business and offer start-up loans, which need to be repaid with interest. Government grants and other financial support may be available. You can get details of these and advice on becoming self-employed from Business Link, a government-funded project for people starting or running a business: www.businesslink.gov. uk, telephone: 0845 600 9006.

WORKING IN EUROPE

British citizens can work in any country that is a member of the European Economic Area (EEA). In general, they have the same employment rights as a citizen of that country or state.

Most self-employed people use an accountant to make sure they pay the correct tax and claim all the possible tax allowances.

Check that you understand:

Equal rights
- the categories covered by the law and exceptions
- equal job/equal pay regardless of gender
- the different commissions working to promote equal opportunities, and
- the grounds for sexual harassment complaints.

At work
- the importance of contracts of employment
- the minimum wage and holiday entitlement, and
- information that has to be provided on pay slips.

Tax
- what is deducted from your earnings and why
- the difference between being self-employed and employed
- where to get help if you need it when filling out forms, and
- the purpose of National Insurance and what happens if you don't pay enough contributions.

Pensions
- who is entitled to a pension, and
- what age men and women can get a pension.

Health and safety
- employer and employee obligations, and
- what to do if you have concerns about health and safety.

Trade unions
- what they are and who can join.

Losing your job
- where to go if you need advice on a problem at work
- possible reasons for dismissal
- the role of Employment Tribunals
- who can help
- the timescale for complaining, and
- entitlement to redundancy pay.

Self-employment
- responsibility for keeping detailed records and paying tax and National Insurance, and
- the role of Business Link.

Childcare and children at work

NEW MOTHERS AND FATHERS

Women who are expecting a baby have a legal right to time off work for antenatal care. They are also entitled to at least 26 weeks' maternity leave. These rights apply to full-time and part-time workers and it makes no difference how long the woman has worked for her employer. It is, however, important to follow the correct procedures and to give the employer enough notice about taking maternity leave. Some women may also be entitled to maternity pay but this depends on how long they have been working for their employer.

Fathers who have worked for their employer for at least 26 weeks are entitled to paternity leave, which provides up to two weeks' time off from work, with pay, when the child is born. It is important to tell your employer well in advance.

You can get advice and more information on maternity and paternity matters from the personnel officer at work, your trade union representative, your local Citizens Advice Bureau, the Citizens Advice Bureau website: www.adviceguide.org.uk or the government website: www.direct.gov.uk

Maternity and paternity leave entitlements have recently changed. For details please see www.lifeintheuk.net. However, for the purposes of your test you must learn the text as reproduced here.

CHILDCARE

It is government policy to help people with childcare responsibilities to take up work. Some employers can help with this. The Childcarelink website www.childcarelink.gov.uk gives information about different types of childcare and registered childminders in your area, or telephone: 08000 96 02 96.

HOURS AND TIME FOR CHILDREN AT WORK

In the UK there are strict laws to protect children from exploitation and to make sure that work does not get in the way of their education. The earliest legal age for children to do paid work is 13, although not all local authorities allow this. There are exceptions for some types of performance work (including modelling) when younger children may be allowed to work. Any child under school-leaving age (16) seeking to do paid work must apply for a licence from the local authority. Children taking part in some kinds of

The earliest legal age a child can work is 13. This statement does not contradict the information on page 34, which says children do not usually work before 14.

performances may have to obtain a medical certificate before working.

By law, children under 16 can only do light work. There are particular jobs that children are not allowed to do. These include delivering milk, selling alcohol, cigarettes or medicines, working in a kitchen or behind the counter of a chip shop, working with dangerous machinery or chemicals, or doing any other kind of work that may be harmful to their health or education.

The law sets out clear limits for the working hours and times for 13- to 16-year-old children. Every child must have at least two consecutive weeks a year during the school holidays when they do not work. They cannot work:

- for more than 4 hours without a one-hour rest break

- for more than 2 hours on any school day or a Sunday

- more than five hours (13- to 14-year-olds) or eight hours (15- to 16-year-olds) on Saturdays (or weekdays during school holidays)

- before 7am or after 7pm

- before the close of school hours (except in areas where local bylaws allow children to work one hour before school)

- for more than 12 hours in any school week, and

- for more than 25 hours a week (13- to 14-year-olds) or 35 hours a week (15- to 16-year-olds) during school holidays.

There is no national minimum wage for those under 16.

By law, children under 16 can only do light work. There are particular jobs that children are not allowed to do.

The local authority may withdraw a child's licence to work, for example where a child works longer hours than the law allows. The child would then be unable to continue to work. An employer may be prosecuted for illegally employing a child. A parent or carer who makes a false declaration in a child's licence application can also be prosecuted. They may also be prosecuted if they do not ensure their child receives a proper education. You can find more information on the TUC website: www.worksmart.org.uk

Check that you understand:

Maternity and paternity rights

- entitlement to maternity leave and pay for both part-time and full-time workers
- paternity leave entitlement, and
- the importance of following the right procedures and providing sufficient notice.

Children at work

- the minimum age for starting work
- the jobs that children under 16 are not allowed to do
- the maximum hours allowed
- the licence and medical certificate requirements
- the local authority's role in licensing and protecting children in employment, and
- parents' responsibilities to ensure that children work within the law and get a proper education.

CHAPTER 7
Extra Revision Notes

➜ IN THIS CHAPTER you'll find some useful summaries of the key terms and dates from chapters 2–6. This includes an extensive glossary of words that you need to know. These are words or phrases that you will need to understand for your test or are terms that you may need to know to give you background to the official study materials. Each word or phrase is explained fully, in easy-to-understand language. As you work your way through the materials, you can use this chapter to check any dates, terms or expressions that are not familiar.

IN THIS CHAPTER THERE IS:

• A timeline of British history
• A British calendar
• A list of words to know

Timeline of British history

This page lists all the key dates in British history that are mentioned in the official study materials.

1530s	Church of England established
1801	First census held in the UK
mid-1840s	Famine in Ireland
1857	Women granted right to divorce
1882	Women granted right to keep earnings and assets when married
1918	Women over 30 granted right to vote
1918	First World War ends
1922	Northern Ireland Parliament established
1928	Women granted right to vote at the same age as men
1939	Second World War begins
1945	Second World War ends
1948	National Health Service (NHS) established
1948	People from Ireland and the West Indies invited to migrate to the UK
1949	Council of Europe created
1957	Treaty of Rome signed and EEC established
1969	Voting age changed to 18
1969	Troubles break out in Northern Ireland
1972	Northern Ireland Parliament abolished
1973	Britain joins the European Union (EU)
1997	Programme to devolve power from central UK Government begins
1999	Creation of the Assembly for Wales and the Scottish Parliament
2001	Last UK census held
2004	Ten new member countries join the EU
2011	Next UK census

British calendar

This page lists all the key dates of the British calendar that are mentioned in the official study materials.

1 January	New Year's Day
14 February	Valentine's Day
1 March	St David's Day
17 March	St Patrick's Day
1 April	April Fool's Day
23 April	St George's Day
31 October	Halloween
5 November	Guy Fawkes Night
11 November	Remembrance Day
30 November	St Andrew's Day
24 December	Christmas Eve
25 December	Christmas Day
26 December	Boxing Day
31 December	Hogmanay

Words to know

Below is a list of terms that are used within the official study materials. You will need to know the meaning of some of the terms for the Life in the UK Test. Other terms have been included as background information to help you understand some of the important concepts and facts in the study guide.

A-levels	A-levels are the examinations taken by students in their last year at school, when aged 18
AS-levels	AS-levels are the examinations taken by students in their second to last year at school, when aged 17
Anglican Church	The Anglican Church is also known as the Church of England
Antenatal care	Medical care given to a woman (and to her unborn baby) while she is pregnant
April Fool's Day	April Fool's Day is the first day in April. People celebrate it by playing jokes on each other
Archbishop of Canterbury	The Archbishop of Canterbury is the head of the **Anglican Church**
Aristocracy	A class of society which enjoys wealth, rank and privilege. Traditionally this is inherited
Asylum	The right to remain in a foreign country granted to someone who would be in danger if they returned to their home country
Bank holidays	Bank holidays are public holidays when banks and most businesses close. They have no religious or national significance
Binge drinking	Binge drinking is drinking alcohol to excess. In recent years, it has become a major focus of concerns about public disorder and minor crime
Bishop	A bishop is a senior figure in a Christian church
Boxing Day	Boxing Day is celebrated on 26 December
British Empire	The British Empire included the countries and lands formerly colonised by Britain in Africa, the Caribbean, North America, Asia and Australasia
Building society	A financial institution, similar to a bank, which is owned by its members (rather than by shareholders) and specialises in providing mortgages and holding deposits for its members
Bureaux de change	A financial service that exchanges currencies from different countries

Bursary	Money in the form of a grant that a university gives to a student to assist them with the costs of their studies
By-election	A by-election is an election held when the representative in a particular constituency either resigns or dies
Cabinet	Cabinet is a committee of about 20 government ministers, chaired by the **Prime Minister**, who meet weekly to decide government policy
Census	The Census is a government survey of the population, held every 10 years, that must be completed by all residents
Chancellor of the Exchequer	The Chancellor of the Exchequer is the minister responsible for economic policy
Chief Moderator	Head of the **Presbyterian Church**
Civil Service	The Civil Service are independent managers and administrators who carry out government policy
Cockney	Cockney is the regional dialect of people who live in London
Commonwealth of Nations	The Commonwealth is an international organisation. It arose out of the remains of the **British Empire**
Compensation	Money which is paid to someone to make up for suffering that they have experienced
Constituency	A constituency is a local area used in elections. People vote for an individual to represent their constituency in the **House of Commons**
Constitution	A constitution is a set of rules for how a country is governed
Coronation	Coronation is the ceremony held when a new monarch is confirmed
Council of Europe	The Council of Europe is made up of most European states. It works to protect human rights and find solutions to European problems
Council of Ministers	The Council of Ministers is made up of ministers from EU states. It proposes new laws and makes decisions about how the EU is run
Credit union	A financial institution, owned and controlled by members, who pool their savings in order to make loans
Day patient	A person who spends several hours during the day in hospital for treatment

Devolved administration	Devolved administration is the principle of central government passing on its powers to regional bodies. This means that decisions about certain government issues can be taken by regional parliaments, such as the **National Assembly for Wales**
Direct debit	A payment (often a bill or membership fee) made from a bank or building society account to an organisation with the express agreement of the account holder
Divorce	Divorce is the legal ending of a marriage
D-plates	Signs attached to a car, in Wales, to indicate that the driver is learning to drive
Dual carriageway	A dual carriageway refers to any road that has physically separated lanes (by either a central barrier or strip of land, known as the central reservation or median)
Electoral register	The electoral register is the list of all people eligible to vote in elections
European Commission	The European Commission is the civil service organisation, based in Brussels, that is responsible for running the activities of the EU
European Economic Community	A former name for the **European Union (EU)**
European Union (EU)	An organisation of 27 member states. It allows members to co-operate, particularly on economic matters
Faith schools	Schools that are linked to a particular religion
Father Christmas	Father Christmas (also known as Santa Claus) is a mythical figure who distributes presents to children at Christmas
First past the post	'First past the post' is the electoral system used in the UK in which the candidate who receives the most votes in a **constituency** wins
Football Association (FA)	The Football Association is responsible for running the game of football in England
Foreign Secretary	The Foreign Secretary is the minister responsible for foreign policy and Britain's relationship with other countries
Free press	Free press means that the media in Britain is not controlled by the government

Gaelic	Gaelic refers to a group of languages. Scottish Gaelic is spoken in parts of Scotland. Irish Gaelic, otherwise known as Irish, is spoken in Northern Ireland and the Republic of Ireland
Gap year	A break from study taken by a young person between school and university, often spent travelling and doing voluntary work
GCSE	An abbreviation for the General Certificate of Secondary Education. GCSE examinations are sat by students at the age of 16
General election	A general election is held at least every five years to elect members of the **House of Commons**
General Practitioner (GP)	A General Practitioner (GP) is a local family doctor who co-ordinates the healthcare a patient receives
Geordie	Geordie is the regional dialect of people who live in Tyneside or Newcastle upon Tyne
Grand National	The Grand National is a horse race held once a year in April
Guy Fawkes Night	Guy Fawkes Night is held annually to celebrate the thwarting of a plot to bomb the Houses of Parliament in 1605
Hansard	Hansard is one of the official records of proceedings in parliament
Hard drugs	Hard drugs are the most serious of illegal drugs, such as heroin, crack, ecstasy and cocaine
Hereditary peers	Hereditary peers used to make up the **House of Lords**. They inherited their places from their parents
Home Secretary	The Home Secretary is the minister responsible for law and order and immigration
House of Commons	The House of Commons is the lower parliamentary assembly where elected **Members of Parliament (MPs)** sit
House of Lords	The House of Lords is the upper parliamentary assembly
Houses of Parliament	The Houses of Parliament is a term used to describe both the **House of Commons** and the **House of Lords**
Independent candidate	An independent candidate is a person who tries to be elected to parliament, but is not a member of a political party
Independent schools	Private schools where all educational costs are met by children's parents
Inpatient	A person who needs to stay overnight for treatment in hospital

Insurance	An arrangement where a company accepts the risk of costs caused by damage to property and other possessions in exchange for regular payments, known as premiums, from the owner
Integrated schools	Schools, in Northern Ireland only, which aim to educate children from different faiths together
Islamic (Sharia) mortgages	A loan for the purchase of a home which does not require interest to be paid
Leader of the Opposition	The Leader of the Opposition is the leader of the second largest party in parliament
Legislation	Legislation is the general name given to all laws
Life Peers	Life Peers are appointed by the **Prime Minister** to sit in the **House of Lords**
Lord Chancellor	The Lord Chancellor is the government minister responsible for legal affairs
L-plates	Signs attached to a car to indicate that the driver is learning to drive
Magistrate	A person who can act as a judge in legal cases involving allegations of minor crime
Maternity leave	A period of time in which a new mother has time off work, in some cases with pay, to give birth and care for her new child
Member of Parliament (MP)	A Member of Parliament is a representative of the people, elected to sit in the **House of Commons**
Metropolitan Police	The Metropolitan Police is the police force that serves the people of London
Minister	A minister is a senior government politician with policy and other responsibilities
Monarch	The Head of State. Used to describe the Queen or King
Mortgage	A loan for the purchase of a home
MOT	A yearly compulsory (Ministry of Transport) test that ensures a vehicle is safe to be driven
Mothering Sunday	Mothering Sunday is a day of celebration where children show appreciation to their mothers
National Assembly for Wales	The National Assembly for Wales is the **devolved administration** which determines certain matters of Welsh policy. It is located in Cardiff

National curriculum	A programme of education, set by the government, that must be followed by schools
National Insurance (NI)	A form of compulsory tax that is used to fund health and welfare services and the **State Pension**
Nationalisation	Where the central government buys, and then controls, a private sector industry or service
New Scotland Yard	New Scotland Yard is the headquarters of the **Metropolitan Police**
Non-departmental public bodies	Non-departmental public bodies are agencies set up and funded by the government. They have greater independence than government departments and are generally allowed to operate without any direct control by the ministers or departments that create them. They are also sometimes known as **quangos**
Northern Ireland Assembly	The Northern Ireland Assembly is the devolved administration which determines certain matters of Northern Irish policy. It is located in Belfast
Off-licence	A shop that sells alcoholic drinks for consumption off the premises (as opposed to a bar or pub)
Outpatient	A person who attends a hospital for treatment for a brief time during the day
Palace of Westminster	The Palace of Westminster, also known as the **Houses of Parliament**, houses the **House of Commons** and the **House of Lords**
Parliament	Parliament is where elected national representatives meet to discuss issues and develop laws
Parliament of Scotland	The Parliament of Scotland, situated in Edinburgh, represents the Scottish people
Parliamentary democracy	A parliamentary democracy is a system of government where decisions are made by a parliament of elected representatives
Party system	A party system is a political system in which representatives and voters organise themselves into groups. These groups usually have shared values and goals
Paternity leave	A period of time when the father of a newly born child may take paid time off work to care for the child
Patron saint	A Christian saint that is traditionally thought to protect a country, or particular group of people

PIN	Personal Identification Number. A code that a person keeps secret that enables them to access money and make purchases using a debit, credit or store card
Presbyterian Church	The Presbyterian Church is the Church of Scotland
Pressure groups	Pressure groups are groups with special interests who seek to influence politicians
Prime Minister	The Prime Minister is the leader of the governing party and chair of the **Cabinet**
Privatisation	Where a private sector company buys, and then controls, a central government industry or service
Proportional representation	Proportional representation is an electoral system, currently used in Scotland, Wales and Northern Ireland, where seats in **parliament** are allocated to parties according to the proportion of votes received
Protestant	A Protestant is a person who belongs to a particular Christian religion. This includes members of the **Anglican Church** and the **Presbyterian Church**
Public office	If you hold a public office you have a job in one of the services or industries managed by the government
Quango	Quango is another name for a **non-departmental public body**
Queen's Speech	The Queen's Speech is delivered by the Queen at the beginning of a new session of parliament setting out government policies and intentions
Redundancy	The loss of a job when the employer no longer needs an employee to perform the particular role or can no longer afford to pay for the role
Reformation	The Reformation was a movement in the 16th century that installed Protestantism as the established religion in Britain
Remembrance Day	Remembrance Day is held each November to remember those who have died at war
Road tax	A tax that must be paid on a vehicle before it can be driven on public roads
R-plates	Signs attached to a car, in Northern Ireland, to indicate that the driver is learning to drive
Scouse	Scouse is the regional dialect of people who live in Liverpool

Shadow Cabinet	The Shadow Cabinet is a group of MPs from the main opposition party in parliament who are responsible for representing the party on important issues
Single carriageway	A single carriageway refers to any road that does not have any physical separation between lanes of opposing flows of traffic. A one-way street is also a single carriageway
Solicitor	A qualified lawyer who gives legal advice and has an important role in the buying and selling of property
Speaker	The Speakers in both the **House of Commons** and **House of Lords** act as chair in parliamentary debates
Standing order	A standing order is an instruction a bank account holder gives to their bank to pay a set amount at regular intervals to another account
State Pension	A regular payment of money by the government to a citizen who has reached retirement age
Stepfamily	A stepfamily is formed when people with children remarry
Stormont	Stormont is the name of the building where the Northern Ireland Assembly meets
Supreme Governor	The Supreme Governor is the role performed by the monarch as head of the **Anglican Church**
Surveyor	A person who provides a check on the condition of a house before it is sold
Tenancy	The period of time that a landlord and tenant agree that a home shall be rented
Tenancy agreement	A legal document that records the agreement reached between a landlord and a tenant to rent a home
Trade union	A group of workers with common interests. It advocates for its members and protects their legal employment rights
The Troubles	A period of violence and political problems in Northern Ireland, especially in the 1960s and 1970s, which happened because Catholic nationalists and Protestant unionists conflicted about whether Northern Ireland should remain part of the UK
United Nations (UN)	The United Nations is a global organisation dedicated to peace, security and human rights
United Nations Security Council	The United Nations Security Council is a committee of 15 member countries focused on global security. The UK is one of five permanent members

Voluntary work	Work that is done without pay, often for a charity
Vulnerable people	People who are disadvantaged in society and may not be able to protect their own interests
Whips	Whips are MPs who ensure other MPs from their political party cast their vote in line with party intentions
Wimbledon	Wimbledon is a prestigious tennis tournament held annually in south London
Yellow Pages	A freely distributed book that lists names, addresses and telephone numbers of businesses, services and organisations in an area

CHAPTER 8
Practice Tests

Preparation tips

→ BEFORE YOU START

The Life in the UK Test is made up of 24 multiple-choice questions. You have 45 minutes to complete the test. This means you have just under two minutes to answer each question. This is plenty of time as long as you concentrate and work steadily. However, don't spend too much time on one question.

Before you begin the test, ask the test supervisor for blank paper. You will not be able to use any other materials during the test. However, you can use the supplied paper to make notes during the test.

If you find a question difficult and are unsure of the correct answer, make a note of the question number on your blank paper. Come back to the question once you have completed the rest of the test.

Questions to expect

All questions in the Life in the UK Test are multiple-choice. There are four different formats in which a question may be asked:

1. One correct answer – Choose the correct answer to the question from four options

   EXAMPLE

   When did women first get the right to vote?

    A 1840

   B 1901

   C 1918

   D 1945

2. Two correct answers – Choose two correct answers to the question from four options

   EXAMPLE

   The UK restricted its immigration laws in the 1970s. However, which TWO locations did Britain admit refugees from during this time?

   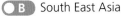 **A** Ethiopia

   B South East Asia

   C Turkey

   D Uganda

3. True or False – Decide whether a statement is true or false

   EXAMPLE

   Is the statement below TRUE or FALSE?

   Judges are independent of the Crown.

    A True

   B False

4. **Select correct statement – Choose the correct statement from two options**

   EXAMPLE
   Which of these statements is correct?

   A The House of Lords may reject laws proposed by the House of Commons.

   B The House of Lords can only delay the passage of new laws.

WORKING THROUGH THE ANSWERS

When you start your test, make sure you read each question carefully. Make sure you understand it.

If you are confident that you know the correct answer, make your selection and move on to the next question.

It is vital that you select an answer for every question even if you are not confident that it is correct. There is a chance that even a guess will be correct! If you do this, make sure that you note the question number on your blank paper. It is possible that a question later in the test will help you to answer a question that you have found difficult.

TRAPS TO WATCH OUT FOR

Some questions may be worded so that an option may be a TRUE statement but not be the CORRECT answer to the question being asked.

Be careful if questions and answers use words that are absolute. These words mean that the question or answer applies in all cases (e.g. always, every) or not at all (e.g. never).

   EXAMPLE
   Which of these statements is correct?

   A The Queen must always marry someone who is Protestant.

   B The Queen must always marry someone who is British.

This question gives the option between two very absolute statements. There are no exceptions. In this example, the correct answer is A. The monarch swears to maintain the Protestant religion in Britain, and must always marry another Protestant.

You also need to be careful of words that *moderate* a question or answer. When words such as *often, rarely, sometimes* and *usually* are used this means that the question or answer is referring to something which is not true in all cases.

EXAMPLE
Where are government statements usually reported as coming from?

 A Buckingham Palace

B Number Ten

C Stormont

D Clarence House

In the above example, it is possible that a government statement might come from other ministers or departments. However, in most cases the media will report most statements as coming from Number Ten. Therefore, option B is the correct answer.

Also watch for negative words in questions or answers – such as *not, never* and *neither.* These words can be easily overlooked and completely change the meaning of the question being asked.

EXAMPLE
Which of the following statements about the Commonwealth is not correct?

A It has a common language

B It has a membership of 53 states

C It has 10% of the world's population

D The Crown is the symbolic head

In the example above, notice that the question is asking for the statement that is not correct. The Commonwealth does have a common language, comprises 53 member states, and the Crown is the symbolic head. The Commonwealth is 30% of the world's population. Therefore, although option C is a false statement, it is the correct answer for this question.

For some questions, one of the answers may read: 'All of the above'. In these cases, read the other answers carefully to see if it is possible that they are all correct. Even if two of the three answers seem correct, all three alternative answers must be correct for you to choose the 'all of the above' option.

For some questions, one of the answers may read: 'None of the above'. In these cases, read the other answers carefully to see if it is possible that they are all incorrect. Even if two of the three answers seem incorrect, all three alternative answers must be wrong for you to choose the 'none of the above' option.

Practice Test 1

1   Is the statement below
    TRUE or FALSE?
    A tenant must leave a home if
    the landlord has a court order
    requiring the tenant to do so.

    A True

    B False

2   How many Assembly Members
    are there in the National
    Assembly for Wales?

    A About 40 members

    B About 30 members

    C About 60 members

    D About 50 members

3   Is the statement below
    TRUE or FALSE?
    *To drink alcohol in a pub,
    you must be 16 or over.*

    A True

    B False

4   Which of these statements
    is correct?

    A A letter of application is a
    short letter that you attach to
    a job application form.

    B A covering letter is a short
    letter that you attach to a job
    application form.

5   Within what period of time
    must a baby be registered
    with the Registrar of Births,
    Marriages and Deaths?

    A Six weeks

    B Twelve months

    C One week

    D Six months

6   What is the second largest party
    in the House of Commons called?

    A The Opposition

    B The Labour Party

    C The Conservation Party

    D Shadow Cabinet

7   How often do most children in the
    UK receive their pocket money?

    A Every day

    B Every week

    C Every month

    D Only on their birthday

8   Is the statement below
    TRUE or FALSE?
    *The Welsh Assembly has
    the power to pass laws
    governing taxation in Wales.*

    A True

    B False

9 When did the Church of England come into existence?

- **A** In the 1640s
- **B** In the 1530s
- **C** In the 1440s
- **D** In the 1750s

10 Which of these statements is correct?

- **A** If you are sexually harassed at work, you should keep a record of the days and times it has occurred.
- **B** If you are sexually harassed at work, you should ignore the problem and hope the harassment stops.

11 What percentage of the UK population say they attend religious services?

- **A** Around 30%
- **B** Around 20%
- **C** Around 10%
- **D** Around 40%

12 Which of the following is not funded by income tax?

- **A** Armed forces
- **B** Rubbish collection
- **C** Police
- **D** Education

13 What is the name of the ministerial position that is responsible for law, order and immigration?

- **A** Home Secretary
- **B** Chief Whip
- **C** Lord Chancellor
- **D** Chancellor of the Exchequer

14 Which of these statements is correct?

- **A** There are a small number of jobs where discrimination laws do not apply.
- **B** All jobs are subject to discrimination laws with no exemptions.

15 Which TWO of the following are important roles of the Prime Minister?

- **A** Appoint the members of the Cabinet
- **B** Effect new laws by giving royal assent to legislation
- **C** Leader of the party in power
- **D** Perform the duties of Head of State

16 Which of these statements is correct?

- **A** A TV licence covers all equipment at one address, even if people rent different rooms in a shared house.
- **B** A TV licence covers all equipment at one address, but people who rent different rooms in a shared house must each buy a separate licence.

17 **Which of the following people do not qualify for free prescriptions in England?**

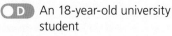 **A** A 30-year-old woman

B A pregnant woman

C A 65-year-old man

D An 18-year-old university student

18 **Which of these statements is correct?**

 A In the 1950s, centres were set up in the West Indies to recruit bus drivers for the UK.

B In the 1950s, centres were set up in Bangladesh to recruit bus drivers for the UK.

19 **Is the statement below TRUE or FALSE?**
People in the UK who buy their own home usually pay for it with a mortgage.

 A True

B False

20 **When is the national day for Scotland?**

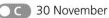 **A** 1 March

B 23 April

C 30 November

D 17 March

21 **If you are buying a home in Scotland, who should you approach first?**

A A bank

B A solicitor

C An estate agent

D Your local MP

22 **Is the statement below TRUE or FALSE?**
By law, radio and television coverage of political parties at election time must give equal time to rival viewpoints.

 A True

B False

23 **What do people wear on Remembrance Day in memory of those who have died at war?**

A Poppies

B Black clothing

C Military clothing

D Red ribbons

24 **What is the current voting age?**

A 21 years old

B 20 years old

C 16 years old

D 18 years old

Answers: Practice Test 1

1	A	True
2	C	About 60 members
3	B	False
4	B	A covering letter is a short letter that you attach to a job application form.
5	A	Six weeks
6	A	The Opposition
7	B	Every week
8	B	False
9	B	In the 1530s
10	A	If you are sexually harassed at work, you should keep a record of the days and times it has occurred.
11	C	Around 10%
12	B	Rubbish collection
13	A	Home Secretary
14	A	There are a small number of jobs where the discrimination laws do not apply.
15	A	Appoint the members of the Cabinet
	C	Leader of the party in power
16	B	A TV licence covers all equipment at one address, but people who rent different rooms in a shared house must each buy a separate licence.
17	A	A 30-year-old woman
18	A	In the 1950s, centres were set up in the West Indies to recruit bus drivers for the UK.
19	A	True
20	C	30 November
21	B	A solicitor
22	A	True
23	A	Poppies
24	D	18 years old

Practice Test 2

1   **Is the statement below TRUE or FALSE?**
Jobcentre Plus provides guidance on who is allowed to work in the UK.

- **A** True
- **B** False

2   **Is the statement below TRUE or FALSE?**
People under 18 cannot drink alcohol in a pub but they can buy it in a supermarket or an off-licence.

- **A** True
- **B** False

3   **When is April Fool's Day?**

- **A** 1 April
- **B** 1 February
- **C** 1 March
- **D** 1 May

4   **Which of these statements is correct?**

- **A** If you have a dispute with your neighbour, you may be able to avoid going to court by using a mediator.
- **B** If you have a dispute with your neighbour, you can only resolve it by going to court.

5   **Which of these statements is correct?**

- **A** Civil servants have to be members of the political party which is in power.
- **B** Civil servants have to be politically neutral and professional.

6   **In England, when do most young people take GCSE examinations?**

- **A** 18 years old
- **B** 16 years old
- **C** 15 years old
- **D** 17 years old

7   **What is the maximum number of hours that children aged 13–16 years old can work in any school week?**

- **A** 8 hours
- **B** 10 hours
- **C** 12 hours
- **D** 14 hours

8   **What percentage of children in the UK live with both birth parents?**

- **A** 25%
- **B** 40%
- **C** 65%
- **D** 80%

9 **Which of these statements is correct?**

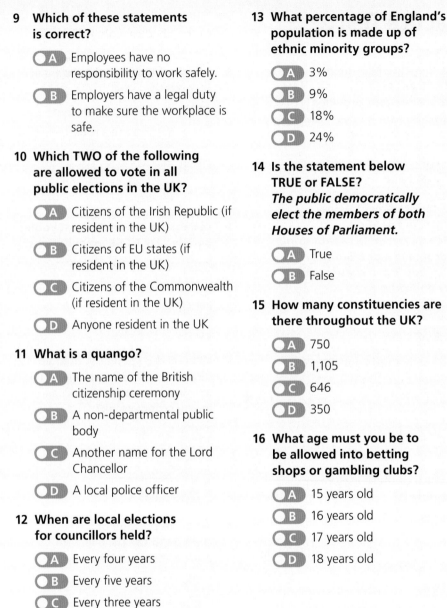

- **A** Employees have no responsibility to work safely.
- **B** Employers have a legal duty to make sure the workplace is safe.

10 **Which TWO of the following are allowed to vote in all public elections in the UK?**

- **A** Citizens of the Irish Republic (if resident in the UK)
- **B** Citizens of EU states (if resident in the UK)
- **C** Citizens of the Commonwealth (if resident in the UK)
- **D** Anyone resident in the UK

11 **What is a quango?**

- **A** The name of the British citizenship ceremony
- **B** A non-departmental public body
- **C** Another name for the Lord Chancellor
- **D** A local police officer

12 **When are local elections for councillors held?**

- **A** Every four years
- **B** Every five years
- **C** Every three years
- **D** May each year

13 **What percentage of England's population is made up of ethnic minority groups?**

- **A** 3%
- **B** 9%
- **C** 18%
- **D** 24%

14 **Is the statement below TRUE or FALSE?**
The public democratically elect the members of both Houses of Parliament.

- **A** True
- **B** False

15 **How many constituencies are there throughout the UK?**

- **A** 750
- **B** 1,105
- **C** 646
- **D** 350

16 **What age must you be to be allowed into betting shops or gambling clubs?**

- **A** 15 years old
- **B** 16 years old
- **C** 17 years old
- **D** 18 years old

17 Where is the Welsh language most widely spoken?

A Ireland

B Wales

C Southern England

D Highlands and Islands of Scotland

18 At what age do young people receive their NI number?

A 18 years old

B 20 years old

C 14 years old

D 16 years old

19 Is the statement below TRUE or FALSE?
It is compulsory for employees to join a trade union.

A True

B False

20 Which of these statements is correct?

A In the 1960s and 1970s, parliament passed laws giving women the right to equal pay.

B In the 1960s and 1970s, parliament passed laws allowing employers to discriminate against women because of their gender.

21 Which politicians are members of the Shadow Cabinet?

A The remaining MPs in government who are not in the Cabinet

B Peers from the House of Lords

C Senior members of the main opposition party

D Civil servants working for the government

22 Is the statement below TRUE or FALSE?
The UK is a member of the EU but not of the Council of Europe.

A True

B False

23 Which of these statements is correct?

A To open a bank account, you will need to provide proof of identity and proof of your current address.

B To open a bank account, you will need only to provide sufficient funds in British currency.

24 How many days a year must a school open?

A 190 days

B 365 days

C 100 days

D 150 days

Answers: Practice Test 2

1	B	False
2	B	False
3	A	1 April
4	A	If you have a dispute with your neighbour then you may be able to avoid going to court by using a mediator.
5	B	Civil servants have to be politically neutral and professional.
6	B	16 years old
7	C	12 hours
8	C	65%
9	B	Employers have a legal duty to make sure the workplace is safe.
10	A	Citizens of the Irish Republic (if resident in the UK)
	C	Citizens of the Commonwealth (if resident in the UK)
11	B	A non-departmental public body
12	D	May each year
13	B	9%
14	B	False
15	C	646
16	D	18 years old
17	B	Wales
18	D	16 years old
19	B	False
20	A	In the 1960s and 1970s, parliament passed laws giving women the right to equal pay.
21	C	Senior members of the main opposition party
22	B	False
23	A	To open a bank account, you will need to provide proof of identity and proof of your current address.
24	A	190 days

17 **What is the name of the police service in Northern Ireland?**

- **A** Police Ombudsman
- **B** Royal Ulster Constabulary
- **C** Police Service of Northern Ireland
- **D** Metropolitan Police

18 **What is a Life Peer?**

- **A** A member of the House of Lords who has been selected by the Prime Minister
- **B** A hereditary aristocrat or peer of the realm
- **C** Any person who has inherited a peerage from their family
- **D** Any person who has served as an MP for more than 20 years

19 **Is the statement below TRUE or FALSE?**
Pressure groups are not allowed to influence government policy.

- **A** True
- **B** False

20 **During the 1950s, where did Britain set up bus driver recruitment centres?**

- **A** Canada
- **B** The West Indies
- **C** Australia
- **D** Ireland

21 **Which TWO of the following are functions of the Speaker of the House of Commons?**

- **A** To give royal assent to new laws agreed in the House of Commons
- **B** To keep order during political debates
- **C** To make sure rules are followed in the House of Commons
- **D** To promote Members from the House of Commons to the House of Lords

22 **Is the statement below TRUE or FALSE?**
University students in England, Wales and Northern Ireland do not have to pay tuition fees.

- **A** True
- **B** False

23 **What is the role of the National Trust?**

- **A** Preserve important buildings and countryside in the UK
- **B** Guarantee a pension for government employees
- **C** Collect the TV licence
- **D** Maintain and enhance the residence of the Prime Minister

24 **Is the statement below TRUE or FALSE?**
All dogs in public places must wear a collar showing the name and address of the owner.

- **A** True
- **B** False

Answers: Practice Test 4

1	A	Uganda
	C	South East Asia
2	D	Council housing
3	A	1 January
	D	25 December
4	B	Citizens Advice Bureau
	D	The housing department of the local authority
5	C	Two-thirds
6	A	GCSE
	C	SQA Standard Grade
7	A	Maternity leave rights apply to both full-time and part-time workers.
8	D	A count of the whole population
9	B	False
10	A	23 April
11	C	1918
12	C	Curriculum vitae
13	D	None – they are all mandatory services provided by local authorities.
14	B	False
15	A	True
16	A	True
17	C	Police Service of Northern Ireland
18	A	A member of the House of Lords who has been selected by the Prime Minister
19	B	False
20	B	The West Indies
21	B	To keep order during political debates
	C	To make sure rules are followed in the House of Commons
22	B	False
23	A	Preserve important buildings and countryside in the UK
24	A	True

Practice Test 5

1 Is the statement below
TRUE or FALSE?
*If you are an adult who
has been unemployed for
18 months, you are usually
required to join New Deal.*

 A True

B False

2 In Wales, what is the name
of the organisation that
provides advice on careers to
children from the age of 11?

A NHS Wales

B Careers Wales

C Wales Connections

D Wales EAL

3 Who is given priority when
GPs visit patients at home?

A Older people

B Pregnant women

C Children under five years old

D People who are unable to
travel

4 Is the statement below
TRUE or FALSE?
*The Northern Ireland Assembly
was established with a power-
sharing agreement between
the main political parties.*

 A True

B False

5 In which TWO of the following
ways can you get tickets
to listen to debates at the
Houses of Parliament?

A Write to your local MP

B Queue at the public entrance

C Book tickets online

D Buy them from nearby ticket
outlets

6 What is the minimum age
that a person must be to be
able to vote in the UK?

A 18

B 19

C 20

D 21

7 How many years must
have passed before an
individual's census form is
viewable by the public?

A 10 years

B 50 years

C 100 years

D An individual's census form
is confidential and never
viewable by the public

8 Is the statement below TRUE or FALSE?
EU citizens living in the UK can vote in general elections.

 A True

B False

9 Who should you call for information about registering for a National Insurance number?

 A National Insurance Registrations Helpline

B NHS Direct

C Your GP

D Your local health authority

10 Who is the current heir to the throne?

A Queen Elizabeth II

B Prince Charles

C Prince Harry

D Prince William

11 Which of these statements is correct?

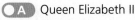 **A** The Metropolitan Police is based at New Scotland Yard.

B The Metropolitan Police is based in the Palace of Westminster.

12 Is the statement below TRUE or FALSE?
In the 1980s, the largest immigrant groups were from the West Indies, India and Pakistan.

 A True

B False

13 Which of these statements is correct?

 A In the UK, women usually have their babies in hospital.

B In the UK, women usually have their babies at home.

14 Is the statement below TRUE or FALSE?
A Prime Minister can be removed from office by their party at any time.

 A True

B False

15 Which TWO of the following do you need to provide to open a bank account?

 A £500

B A work permit

C Proof of your address

D Proof of your identity

16 Which of these statements is correct?

A A woman's entitlement to maternity leave depends on how long she has been working for her employer.

B A woman's entitlement to maternity pay depends on how long she has been working for her employer.

17 Is the statement below TRUE or FALSE?
European Union law is legally binding in the UK.

- **A** True
- **B** False

18 Which of these statements is correct?

- **A** A judge can decide whether a person is guilty or innocent of a serious crime.
- **B** A judge can only decide on the penalty for a person found guilty of a serious crime.

19 What percentage of London's population is made up of ethnic minorities?

- **A** 45% of London's population
- **B** 29% of London's population
- **C** 9% of London's population
- **D** 15% of London's population

20 Which TWO of the following mean that you might be entitled to redundancy pay?

- **A** If you are dismissed from your job
- **B** If you meet performance targets set by your employer
- **C** The employer cannot afford to pay for the job
- **D** The job is no longer needed by the employer

21 According to the 2001 census, what proportion of the UK population are Christians?

- **A** Two people out of ten
- **B** Seven people out of ten
- **C** Five people out of ten
- **D** Nine people out of ten

22 How much money will a landlord usually ask for as a deposit at the beginning of a tenancy?

- **A** An amount equal to one week's rent
- **B** An amount equal to two week's rent
- **C** An amount equal to three week's rent
- **D** An amount equal to one month's rent

23 What is the population of England?

- **A** About 60 million
- **B** About 50 million
- **C** About 40 million
- **D** About 30 million

24 When is Guy Fawkes Night?

- **A** The evening of 15 October
- **B** The evening of 30 May
- **C** The evening of 5 November
- **D** The evening of 25 September

Answers: Practice Test 5

1	A	True
2	B	Careers Wales
3	D	People who are unable to travel
4	A	True
5	A	Write to your local MP
	B	Queue at the public entrance
6	A	18
7	C	100 years
8	B	False
9	A	National Insurance Registrations Helpline
10	B	Prince Charles
11	A	The Metropolitan Police is based at New Scotland Yard.
12	B	False
13	A	In the UK, women usually have their babies in hospital.
14	A	True
15	C	Proof of your address
	D	Proof of your identity
16	B	A woman's entitlement to maternity pay depends on how long she has been working for her employer.
17	A	True
18	B	A judge can only decide on the penalty for a person found guilty of a serious crime.
19	B	29% of London's population
20	C	The employer cannot afford to pay for the job
	D	The job is no longer needed by the employer
21	B	Seven people out of ten
22	D	An amount equal to one month's rent.
23	B	About 50 million
24	C	The evening of 5 November

Practice Test 6

1 **Is the statement below TRUE or FALSE?**
The Council of Ministers, together with the European Parliament, is the legislative body of the European Union.

- **A** True
- **B** False

2 **When was the Second World War?**

- **A** 1840–1846
- **B** 1901–1918
- **C** 1939–1945
- **D** 1919–1925

3 **Which of these statements is correct?**

- **A** The HM Revenue & Customs self-assessment helpline can provide help and advice on filling out tax forms.
- **B** You can only get help filling out tax forms by paying for the services of an accountant.

4 **Which of these statements is correct?**

- **A** Your pay slip only needs to show how much money has been taken off for tax.
- **B** Your pay slip must show how much money has been taken off for tax and National Insurance contributions.

5 **Which government department is responsible for collecting taxes?**

- **A** Ministry of Defence
- **B** Department of Health
- **C** HM Revenue & Customs
- **D** Financial Services Authority

6 **What percentage of children do not live with both birth parents?**

- **A** 65%
- **B** 35%
- **C** 25%
- **D** 10%

7 **Which minister can sit in the House of Lords or in the House of Commons?**

- **A** Foreign Secretary
- **B** Home Secretary
- **C** Lord Chancellor
- **D** Chancellor of the Exchequer

8 **Through which TWO of the following do you make an offer on a home you want to buy?**

- **A** A bank
- **B** A GP
- **C** A solicitor
- **D** An estate agent

9 Is the statement below
   TRUE or FALSE?
   *The number of people migrating
   to Britain from the West
   Indies, India, Pakistan and
   Bangladesh increased over the
   late 1960s and early 1970s.*

    A   True

   B   False

10 For which TWO reasons can an
    employer can give you a warning?

    A   Being sick

    B   You are unacceptably late for
        work

    C   You cannot do your job
        properly

    D   Missing work because of a
        family bereavement

11 Which of these statements
    is correct?

    A   It is illegal to mistreat an
        animal.

    B   Mistreating an animal is
        unethical but not against the
        law.

12 When looking for employment,
    what is the purpose of a referee?

    A   To write a report about a
        person's suitability for a job

    B   To search for jobs that match
        your skills

    C   To negotiate pay after a
        successful interview

    D   To resolve any disputes between
        you and your employer

13 In which TWO UK elections
    can European citizens vote?

    A   Elections to the House of Lords

    B   European elections

    C   Local elections

    D   National elections

14 Is the statement below
    TRUE or FALSE?
    *After the age of 70, drivers
    must renew their driving licence
    for three years at a time.*

     A   True

    B   False

15 Is the statement below
    TRUE or FALSE?
    *Hereditary peers have lost
    the automatic right to attend
    the House of Lords.*

    A   True

    B   False

16 Is the statement below
    TRUE or FALSE?
    *Everything you tell your GP is
    confidential and cannot be passed
    on without your permission.*

    A   True

    B   False

17 Is the statement below
    TRUE or FALSE?
    *In the UK, both the birth rate
    and the death rate are falling.*

    A   True

    B   False

18 Is the statement below TRUE or FALSE?
Independent schools are paid for by the state.

 A True

B False

19 Which TWO of the following answers could you use to prove your identity when opening a bank or building society account?

A Your passport or driving licence

B A signed photograph or National Insurance number card

C Your birth certificate or marriage certificate

D Your tenancy agreement or a household bill in your name that shows your address

20 Is the statement below TRUE or FALSE?
Volunteering can provide you with useful experience that can help with future job applications.

A True

B False

21 How are Whips appointed?

 A By the Prime Minister

B By vote amongst their peers

C By the King or Queen

D By their party leaders

22 Which TWO of the following jobs are children under 16 not allowed to do?

A Selling alcohol

B Delivering newspapers

C Working behind the counter of a chip shop

D Dog walking

23 What is the minimum age required to drive a car?

A 17 years old

B 16 years old

C 18 years old

D 21 years old

24 At what age can women get a State Pension?

A 60 years old

B 65 years old

C 55 years old

D 70 years old

Answers: Practice Test 6

1	A	True
2	C	1939–1945
3	A	The HM Revenue & Customs self-assessment helpline can provide help and advice on filling out tax forms.
4	B	Your pay slip must show how much money has been taken off for tax and National Insurance contributions.
5	C	HM Revenue & Customs
6	B	35%
7	C	Lord Chancellor
8	C	A solicitor
	D	An estate agent
9	B	False
10	B	You are unacceptably late for work
	C	You cannot do your job properly
11	A	It is illegal to mistreat an animal.
12	A	To write a report about a person's suitability for a job
13	B	European elections
	C	Local elections
14	A	True
15	A	True
16	A	True
17	A	True
18	B	False
19	A	Your passport or driving licence
	D	Your tenancy agreement or a household bill in your name that shows your address
20	A	True
21	D	By their party leaders
22	A	Selling alcohol
	C	Working behind the counter of a chip shop
23	A	17 years old
24	A	60 years old

Practice Test 7

1 Is the statement below TRUE or FALSE?
The Prime Minister usually resigns when their party is defeated in a general election.

- **A** True
- **B** False

2 Which of these statements is correct?

- **A** Trade unions are organisations that aim to improve the pay and working conditions of their members.
- **B** Trade unions work to protect the interests of employers.

3 For what reason could you be immediately dismissed from your job?

- **A** Because of your sexuality
- **B** Because of your age
- **C** Because of your religious beliefs
- **D** Because of serious misconduct

4 Is the statement below TRUE or FALSE?
In the UK, it is illegal to be drunk in public.

- **A** True
- **B** False

5 What is the distance from John O'Groats on the north coast of Scotland to Land's End in the south-west corner of England?

- **A** Approximately 1,100 miles (1,770 kilometres)
- **B** Approximately 500 miles (800 kilometres)
- **C** Approximately 870 miles (1,400 kilometres)
- **D** Approximately 1,310 miles (2,110 kilometres)

6 Which of these statements is correct?

- **A** AGCEs used to be called AS-levels.
- **B** AGCEs used to be called A-levels.

7 Is the statement below TRUE or FALSE?
Somebody aged 16 can drink wine or beer with a meal in a hotel or restaurant.

- **A** True
- **B** False

8 Which TWO of the following are names that can be used to refer to the Church of England?

- **A** Baptist Church
- **B** Episcopal Church
- **C** Anglican Church
- **D** Presbyterian Church

9 Is the statement below TRUE or FALSE?
Very few people believe that women in Britain should stay at home and not go out to paid work.

 A True

B False

10 Which of these statements is correct?

A The National Curriculum includes subjects such as English, maths and science but excludes modern foreign languages, art and music.

B The National Curriculum includes subjects such as English, maths, science, modern foreign languages, art and music.

11 Who were Suffragettes?

A Campaigners for greater rights for women

B Refugee care workers

C Representatives of people seeking asylum

D Nurses who cared for the elderly

12 How often is the electoral register updated?

A Every five years

B Every year

C Every two years

D Every time somebody moves house

13 How often does the Cabinet normally meet?

A Monthly

B Bi-weekly

C Daily

D Weekly

14 Which tradition is observed on 31 October?

A Mother's Day

B Guy Fawkes Night

C Halloween

D St Andrew's Day

15 Is the statement below TRUE or FALSE?
It is estimated that half of young people have taken part in fund-raising or collecting money for charity.

A True

B False

16 According to the 2001 census, what percentage of people stated their religion as Muslim?

A Approximately 21%

B Approximately 1%

C Approximately 3%

D Approximately 15%

17 **Is the statement below**
TRUE or FALSE?
The House of Commons
cannot overrule the decisions
of the House of Lords.

- **A** True
- **B** False

18 **If your child's main language is**
not English, they can get extra
support from a specialist teacher.
What is this teacher called?

- **A** PAL teacher
- **B** ESE teacher
- **C** EAL teacher
- **D** LLL teacher

19 **What is the purpose**
of a NI number?

- **A** To prove that you have British
nationality
- **B** To track National Insurance
contributions
- **C** To allow companies to check
your credit history
- **D** To prove that you have
adequate home insurance

20 **At what ages are Key Stage**
tests held in England?

- **A** 10, 12 and 14
- **B** 7, 11 and 14
- **C** 7 and 15
- **D** 11, 15 and 17

21 **What do the initials**
GCSE stand for?

- **A** Grade Certificate of Secondary
Education
- **B** General Certificate of Scottish
Education
- **C** General Certificate of
Secondary Education
- **D** Grade Certificate of Scottish
Education

22 **Is the statement below**
TRUE or FALSE?
You cannot be arrested if you
refuse to take a breathalyser test.

- **A** True
- **B** False

23 **Which of these statements**
is correct?

- **A** An individual's census
information is released
immediately after the census
is completed for the public to
search.
- **B** An individual's census
information is kept confidential
and anonymous for 100 years.

24 **Which TWO of the following**
should you speak to if you have
trouble with your neighbours?

- **A** The bank
- **B** The local authority
- **C** Your GP
- **D** Your landlord

Answers: Practice Test 7

1	A	True
2	A	Trade unions are organisations that aim to improve the pay and working conditions of their members.
3	D	Because of serious misconduct
4	A	True
5	C	Approximately 870 miles (1,400 kilometres)
6	B	AGCEs used to be called A-levels.
7	A	True
8	B	Episcopal Church
	C	Anglican Church
9	A	True
10	B	The National Curriculum includes subjects such as English, maths, science, modern foreign languages, art and music.
11	A	Campaigners for greater rights for women
12	B	Every year
13	D	Weekly
14	C	Halloween
15	A	True
16	C	Approximately 3%
17	B	False
18	C	EAL teacher
19	B	To track National Insurance contributions
20	B	7, 11 and 14
21	C	General Certificate of Secondary Education
22	B	False
23	B	An individual's census information is kept confidential and anonymous for 100 years.
24	B	The local authority
	D	Your landlord

Practice Test 8

1 Which of these statements is correct?

 A Over 50% of young people in the UK take part in community events.

B Few young people in the UK take part in community events.

2 Is the statement below TRUE or FALSE?
Women are only entitled to maternity leave after they have completed their first year in a job.

A True

B False

3 Which of these statements is correct?

A To see a doctor, you must call NHS Direct to arrange an appointment.

B To see a doctor, you must make an appointment at your GP surgery or visit an NHS walk-in centre.

4 Which of these statements is correct?

A Children must apply for a National Insurance number when they get their first job.

B Children receive their National Insurance number just before their 16th birthday.

5 Is the statement below TRUE or FALSE?
Scots is the name of the old Scottish language.

A False

B True

6 When should you look for a GP?

A Once you have registered with the local authority

B When you become ill

C As soon as you move to a new area

D When you visit the local hospital

7 When is Boxing Day?

A 26 December

B 25 December

C 31 December

D 1 January

8 From which TWO of the following options can you learn about training opportunities?

A Local library

B Local MP

C Learndirect

D Local sports club

9   What is the minimum age for purchasing alcohol from a supermarket or off-licence?

- Ⓐ 17 years old
- Ⓑ 18 years old
- Ⓒ 16 years old
- Ⓓ 14 years old

10   Which of the UK national days is celebrated with a public holiday?

- Ⓐ St Patrick's Day in Northern Ireland
- Ⓑ St Andrew's Day in Scotland
- Ⓒ St George's Day in England
- Ⓓ St David's Day in Wales

11   What percentage of the workforce are women?

- Ⓐ 40%
- Ⓑ 45%
- Ⓒ 51%
- Ⓓ 65%

12   Which other name can be used to refer to the Church of England?

- Ⓐ The Methodist Church
- Ⓑ The Catholic Church
- Ⓒ The Presbyterian Church
- Ⓓ The Anglican Church

13   When did women in the UK first get the right to vote?

- Ⓐ 1888
- Ⓑ 1918
- Ⓒ 1928
- Ⓓ 1945

14   Which of these statements is correct?

- Ⓐ If you want to drive a car but only have a provisional driving licence, you must be accompanied by someone who is over the age of 21 and has held (and still holds) a full licence for more than one year.
- Ⓑ If you want to drive a car but only have a provisional driving licence, you must be accompanied by someone who is over the age of 21 and has held (and still holds) a full licence for three years.

15   What is the largest ethnic minority in Britain?

- Ⓐ Indian descent
- Ⓑ Black Caribbean descent
- Ⓒ Pakistani descent
- Ⓓ Bangladeshi descent

16   Which TWO of the following happen if you do not pay enough National Insurance contributions?

- Ⓐ You may not receive a full state retirement pension
- Ⓑ You will be fined and need to sign up to a repayment plan
- Ⓒ You will be prosecuted and may face a prison sentence
- Ⓓ You will not be entitled to certain benefits such as Jobseeker's Allowance or maternity pay

17 Which of these statements is correct?

- **A** You may use a driving licence or recent phone bill to prove identity.
- **B** An identity card is the only document that can be used to prove your identity.

18 Where is the Prime Minister's official residence?

- **A** 10 Downing Street
- **B** 12 Downing Street
- **C** Palace of Westminster
- **D** Buckingham Palace

19 Is the statement below TRUE or FALSE?
More people attend religious services in Scotland and Northern Ireland than in England and Wales.

- **A** True
- **B** False

20 From which TWO of the following places can you get advice and information for setting up your own business?

- **A** Jobcentre Plus
- **B** Home Office
- **C** Business Link
- **D** Banks

21 Is the statement below TRUE or FALSE?
It is possible to open bank accounts in some supermarkets or on the internet.

- **A** True
- **B** False

22 Is the statement below TRUE or FALSE?
In Northern Ireland, many secondary schools select children through a test taken at the age of 11.

- **A** True
- **B** False

23 Which TWO of the following options can provide you with health advice and treatment while you are pregnant and after you have had a baby?

- **A** Your GP or local health authority
- **B** Family Planning Association
- **C** Health visitor
- **D** Local nursery

24 How old must you be to drink alcohol with a meal in a hotel or restaurant?

- **A** 16 years old
- **B** 17 years old
- **C** 18 years old
- **D** 19 years old

Answers: Practice Test 8

1	A	Over 50% of young people in the UK take part in community events.
2	B	False
3	B	To see a doctor you must make an appointment at your GP surgery or visit an NHS walk-in centre.
4	B	Children receive their National Insurance number just before their 16th birthday.
5	B	True
6	C	As soon as you move to a new area
7	A	26 December
8	A	Local library
	C	Learndirect
9	B	18 years old
10	A	St Patrick's Day in Northern Ireland
11	B	45%
12	D	The Anglican Church
13	B	1918
14	B	If you want to drive a car but only have a provisional driving licence, you must be accompanied by someone who is over the age of 21 and has held (and still holds) a full licence for three years.
15	A	Indian descent
16	A	You may not receive a full state retirement pension
	D	You will not be entitled to certain benefits such as Jobseeker's Allowance or maternity pay
17	A	You may use a driving licence or recent phone bill to prove identity.
18	A	10 Downing Street
19	A	True
20	C	Business Link
	D	Banks
21	A	True
22	A	True
23	A	Your GP or local health authority
	C	Health visitor
24	A	16 years old

Practice Test 9

1 Which TWO of the following do trade unions aim to achieve for their members?

- **A** Provide advice and support on problems at work
- **B** Deduct tax from their earnings
- **C** Improve their pay and working conditions
- **D** Limit overall pay increases

2 Is the statement below TRUE or FALSE?
If you have problems with your neighbours, you should contact the police for details of mediation organisations that help neighbours to solve their disputes.

- **A** True
- **B** False

3 Which TWO of the following are funded by National Insurance contributions?

- **A** Local council services
- **B** National Health Service
- **C** Defence forces
- **D** State Pension

4 Which of the following are TWO places that can provide you with information about maternity and paternity leave?

- **A** Personnel officer at work
- **B** NHS Direct
- **C** ChildcareLink
- **D** Citizens Advice Bureau

5 How much of the money for local authority services is raised through council tax?

- **A** 10%
- **B** 20%
- **C** 25%
- **D** 35%

6 When did 12 European states adopt the euro as a common currency?

- **A** 1995
- **B** 2002
- **C** 2000
- **D** 1980

7 Which of the following statements regarding the Commonwealth is not correct?

- **A** Membership is compulsory
- **B** It aims to promote democracy
- **C** It has no power over its members
- **D** It can suspend the membership of a country

8 Which of these statements is correct?

- **A** Citizens of EU states who are resident in the UK cannot vote in national parliamentary elections.
- **B** Citizens of EU states who are resident in the UK can vote in all public elections.

9 Who is responsible for organising the health treatment you receive?

- **A** Your GP
- **B** A specialist
- **C** The local authority
- **D** Your local MP

10 What is the charge for the supply of water to a home called?

- **A** Supply rates
- **B** Piping charge
- **C** Income tax
- **D** Water rates

11 Which country of the UK has the highest proportion of ethnic minority groups in its population?

- **A** Scotland
- **B** England
- **C** Northern Ireland
- **D** Wales

12 Is the statement below TRUE or FALSE?
Insurance for a car or motorcycle is optional.

- **A** True
- **B** False

13 Which of these statements is correct?

- **A** Women have always had the same rights as men.
- **B** In 19th-century Britain, women had fewer rights than men.

14 What proportion of women with children (of school age) are in paid work?

- **A** Half
- **B** Two-thirds
- **C** One-quarter
- **D** Three-quarters

15 How is it decided which party forms the government?

- **A** The party with the most votes forms the government
- **B** The party with the most candidates forms the government
- **C** The party that wins the majority of constituencies forms the government
- **D** The members of the House of Lords vote for their preferred party

16 Is the statement below
TRUE or FALSE?
Most of the laws protecting
people at work apply equally
to people doing part-
time or full-time jobs.

- **A** True
- **B** False

17 What proportion of young
people in the UK go on
to higher education?

- **A** One in two
- **B** One in three
- **C** One in four
- **D** One in five

18 Is the statement below
TRUE or FALSE?
Everyone in the UK is
allowed to work.

- **A** True
- **B** False

19 Who from the list below is
not responsible for controlling
the finances of the police?

- **A** Councillors
- **B** Police Ombudsman
- **C** The government
- **D** Magistrates

20 Which of these statements
is correct?

- **A** All dentists work for the NHS.
- **B** Some dentists have two sets
  of charges, both NHS and
  private.

21 On which TWO of the following
matters can the Scottish
Parliament make decisions?

- **A** Defence
- **B** Education
- **C** Foreign Policy
- **D** Health

22 Is the statement below
TRUE or FALSE?
Britain was a founding
member of the EU.

- **A** True
- **B** False

23 Hogmanay is a traditional
celebration in which country?

- **A** England
- **B** Wales
- **C** Scotland
- **D** Northern Ireland

24 What is the youngest legal age
for children to do paid work?

- **A** 11 years old
- **B** 12 years old
- **C** 13 years old
- **D** 14 years old

Answers: Practice Test 9

1	A	Provide advice and support on problems at work
	C	Improve their pay and working conditions
2	B	False
3	B	National Health Service
	D	State Pension
4	A	Personnel officer at work
	D	Citizens Advice Bureau
5	B	20%
6	B	2002
7	A	Membership is compulsory
8	A	Citizens of EU states who are resident in the UK cannot vote in national parliamentary elections.
9	A	Your GP
10	D	Water rates
11	B	England
12	B	False
13	B	In 19th-century Britain, women had fewer rights than men.
14	D	Three-quarters
15	C	The party that wins the majority of constituencies forms the government
16	A	True
17	B	One in three
18	B	False
19	B	Police Ombudsman
20	B	Some dentists have two sets of charges, both NHS and private.
21	B	Education
	D	Health
22	B	False
23	C	Scotland
24	C	13 years old

Practice Test 10

1   What is the UK's role within the UN?

- **A** Member of the UN Security Council
- **B** Selects the UN Secretary General from members of the Security Council
- **C** Provides a neutral location for hosting UN meetings in Scotland
- **D** All of the above

2   When is a jury used?

- **A** To choose an appropriate penalty for someone found guilty of a serious crime
- **B** To confirm decisions made by a judge
- **C** To decide if someone is innocent or guilty of a less important crime
- **D** To decide if someone is innocent or guilty of a serious crime

3   Is the statement below TRUE or FALSE?
Discounts on train tickets are available for people over 60 years of age.

- **A** False
- **B** True

4   Is the statement below TRUE or FALSE?
Cigarette consumption by adults in Britain has risen significantly.

- **A** False
- **B** True

5   What is the minimum age to be able to drink alcohol in a pub?

- **A** 16 years old
- **B** 21 years old
- **C** 18 years old
- **D** It depends if you are with an adult

6   Is the statement below TRUE or FALSE?
There is no United Kingdom football team. Each country has its own national team.

- **A** True
- **B** False

7   How can you compare qualifications from another country with those in the UK?

- **A** By visiting your local library
- **B** By contacting the National Academic Recognition Information Centre
- **C** By writing to potential employers
- **D** By asking your neighbour

8 At what age can men get a State Pension?

- Ⓐ 55 years old
- Ⓑ 60 years old
- Ⓒ 70 years old
- Ⓓ 65 years old

9 When were women over 30 given the right to vote?

- Ⓐ 1918
- Ⓑ 1945
- Ⓒ 1901
- Ⓓ 1840

10 Which of these statements is correct?

- Ⓐ You have to pay a small charge to visit your local GP.
- Ⓑ Treatment from your local GP is free.

11 Which of these statements is correct?

- Ⓐ It is illegal to discriminate against someone for employment in any circumstances.
- Ⓑ Discrimination is not against the law when the job involves working for someone in their own home.

12 Which TWO of the following are roles of the Whips in parliament?

- Ⓐ Ensure attendance of MPs at voting time in the House of Commons
- Ⓑ Ensure the House of Commons is always safe and secure
- Ⓒ Keep order in the House of Commons during political debates
- Ⓓ Responsible for discipline in their party

13 Is the statement below TRUE or FALSE?
Members of the public are not able to visit the Houses of Parliament.

- Ⓐ True
- Ⓑ False

14 How long was Britain at war during the Second World War?

- Ⓐ Four years
- Ⓑ Eight years
- Ⓒ Two years
- Ⓓ Six years

15 Is the statement below TRUE or FALSE?
People borrowing money from banks to pay for cars and holidays is more common in the UK than in many other countries.

- Ⓐ True
- Ⓑ False

16 What is the difference in the average hourly pay rate for men and women?

 A The average hourly pay rate is 5% lower for women

B The average hourly pay rate is 10% lower for women

C The average hourly pay rate is 20% lower for women

D No difference – the average hourly pay rate for women is the same as men

17 Which TWO of the following groups do not have to pay for eye sight tests?

A People living in in Scotland

B People over 60 years old

C People living in England

D People with a full-time job

18 Is the statement below TRUE or FALSE?
In primary schools, boys and girls usually learn together.

A True

B False

19 When will women have the same pension age as men?

A 2010

B 2015

C 2020

D 2025

20 When are general elections held?

A At least every year

B At least every four years

C At least every five years

D At least every ten years

21 What is the estimated population of the UK?

A About 60 million

B About 50 million

C About 80 million

D About 40 million

22 Which TWO of the following are functions of the House of Lords?

A Elect the Prime Minister

B Elect the Speaker of the House of Commons

C Propose new laws

D Suggest amendments to laws

23 Which of these statements is correct?

A The Council of the European Union is the governing body of the EU.

B The Council of Europe is the governing body of the EU.

24 Is the statement below TRUE or FALSE?
If you are the tenant of a property then you do not have to pay council tax.

A True

B False

Answers: Practice Test 10

1	A	Member of the UN Security Council
2	D	To decide if someone is innocent or guilty of a serious crime
3	B	True
4	A	False
5	C	18 years old
6	A	True
7	B	By contacting the National Academic Recognition Information Centre
8	D	65 years old
9	A	1918
10	B	Treatment from your local GP is free.
11	B	Discrimination is not against the law when the job involves working for someone in their own home.
12	A	Ensure attendance of MPs at voting time in the House of Commons
	D	Responsible for discipline in their party
13	B	False
14	D	Six years
15	A	True
16	C	The average hourly pay rate is 20% lower for women
17	A	You live in Scotland
	B	You are over 60 years old
18	A	True
19	C	2020
20	C	At least every five years
21	A	About 60 million
22	C	Propose new laws
	D	Suggest amendments to laws
23	A	The Council of the European Union is the governing body of the EU.
24	B	False

Practice Test 11

1 What is a civil servant?

- **A** A manager or administrator who works for the House of Lords
- **B** A manager or administrator who carries out government policy
- **C** A member of a political party
- **D** A Member of Parliament

2 Is the statement below TRUE or FALSE?
Someone is more likely to be elected as an MP if they have been nominated to represent a major political party.

- **A** True
- **B** False

3 When does Prime Minister's Questions take place?

- **A** Every day while parliament is sitting
- **B** Once a week while parliament is sitting
- **C** Once every fortnight while parliament is sitting
- **D** On the first day of each month

4 Is the statement below TRUE or FALSE?
The Queen must not marry anyone who is not Protestant.

- **A** True
- **B** False

5 In which TWO of the following places can you read copies of Hansard?

- **A** Newspapers
- **B** Television
- **C** Large libraries
- **D** Internet

6 Is the statement below TRUE or FALSE?
In the early 1970s, the government passed new laws which restricted immigration but these new laws did not apply to immigrants from Australia, New Zealand and Canada.

- **A** True
- **B** False

7 What is the second largest religious group in the UK?

- **A** Jewish
- **B** Buddhist
- **C** Sikh
- **D** Muslim

8 Between what ages can women claim Jobseeker's Allowance?

- **A** 21–65 years old
- **B** 18–60 years old
- **C** 18–65 years old
- **D** 16–65 years old

9   **What are courses for people who want to improve their English language skills called?**

- Ⓐ NHS
- Ⓑ EEE
- Ⓒ ESOL
- Ⓓ EAL

10   **Which of the following are pressure groups?**

- Ⓐ Trade unions
- Ⓑ Government departments
- Ⓒ Select committees
- Ⓓ Political parties

11   **Which TWO of the following can act as a referee when you apply for a job?**

- Ⓐ Your father
- Ⓑ Your employer
- Ⓒ Your tutor
- Ⓓ A friend

12   **Is the statement below TRUE or FALSE?**
Independent secondary schools are sometimes called public schools.

- Ⓐ True
- Ⓑ False

13   **Which of these statements is correct?**

- Ⓐ All housing in Northern Ireland is provided by the Northern Ireland Housing Executive.
- Ⓑ Social housing in Northern Ireland is provided by the Northern Ireland Housing Executive.

14   **What does Remembrance Day commemorate?**

- Ⓐ The crucifixion of Jesus Christ
- Ⓑ The appreciation of single mothers
- Ⓒ The celebration of community
- Ⓓ The memory of those who died fighting in wars

15   **How many members are there in the Northern Ireland Assembly?**

- Ⓐ 82 members
- Ⓑ 64 members
- Ⓒ 108 members
- Ⓓ 125 members

16   **When was the Council of Europe established?**

- Ⓐ 1964
- Ⓑ 1901
- Ⓒ 1982
- Ⓓ 1949

17 What do people sometimes do on Valentine's Day?

- A Wear poppies in memory of St Valentine
- B Fast from eating for the whole day
- C Play jokes on each other until midday
- D Send anonymous cards to someone they secretly admire

18 When is St Patrick's Day celebrated?

- A 1 March
- B 17 March
- C 23 April
- D 30 November

19 What must a candidate achieve in order to win their constituency?

- A Win the most votes out of all candidates in their constituency
- B Win at least 15,000 votes
- C Be a member of the party that wins government office
- D Win at least 25% of the votes within their constituency

20 Is the statement below TRUE or FALSE?
The employment of children in the UK is strictly controlled by law.

- A True
- B False

21 Which of these statements is correct?

- A If you lose your job because the company you work for no longer has a need for your job, you may be entitled to redundancy pay.
- B If you lose your job because the company you work for no longer has a need for your job, you are not entitled to redundancy pay.

22 Is the statement below TRUE or FALSE?
British citizens require a work permit before they can work in any country that is a member of the European Economic Area.

- A True
- B False

23 Is the statement below TRUE or FALSE?
Members of the public are not able to visit the Scottish Parliament.

- A True
- B False

24 Where should you go for help if you are homeless?

- A To the local authority
- B To the local hospital
- C To your GP
- D To your MP

Answers: Practice Test 11

1	B	A manager or administrator who carries out government policy
2	A	True
3	B	Once a week while parliament is sitting
4	A	True
5	C	Large libraries
	D	Internet
6	A	True
7	D	Muslim
8	B	18–60 years old
9	C	ESOL
10	A	Trade unions
11	B	Your employer
	C	Your tutor
12	A	True
13	B	Social housing in Northern Ireland is provided by the Northern Ireland Housing Executive.
14	D	The memory of those who died fighting in wars
15	C	108 members
16	D	1949
17	D	Send anonymous cards to someone they secretly admire
18	B	17 March
19	A	Win the most votes out of all candidates in their constituency
20	A	True
21	A	If you lose your job because the company you work for no longer has a need for your job, you may be entitled to redundancy pay.
22	B	False
23	B	False
24	A	To the local authority

Practice Test 12

1 What percentage of children live within a stepfamily?

- **A** 10%
- **B** 25%
- **C** 40%
- **D** 55%

2 Between what ages can men claim Jobseeker's Allowance?

- **A** 21–65 years old
- **B** 18–60 years old
- **C** 16–65 years old
- **D** 18–65 years old

3 Which TWO subjects are included in Skills for Life courses in England and Wales?

- **A** Metalwork
- **B** ESOL
- **C** Arts and crafts
- **D** Numeracy

4 Is the statement below TRUE or FALSE?
If you are an adult who has been unemployed for six months then you are usually required to join New Deal to continue receiving benefits.

- **A** True
- **B** False

5 What does Christmas Day celebrate?

- **A** The miracles of Jesus Christ
- **B** The birth of Jesus Christ
- **C** The resurrection of Jesus Christ
- **D** The death of Jesus Christ

6 Is the statement below TRUE or FALSE?
Foreign currency can only be bought or changed at post offices.

- **A** True
- **B** False

7 What is the title of the most senior representative in the Church of Scotland?

- **A** Moderator
- **B** Supreme Governor
- **C** Archbishop of Canterbury
- **D** Archbishop of Edinburgh

8 How many independent schools are there in the UK?

- **A** 100
- **B** 1,000
- **C** 2,500
- **D** 15,000

9   Is the statement below TRUE or FALSE?
Despite existing laws, women still do not always have the same access to promotion and better paid jobs as men.

- **A** False
- **B** True

10   Is the statement below TRUE or FALSE?
The minimum wage rate is the same for everyone.

- **A** True
- **B** False

11   At what age do school children take their first national test in Wales?

- **A** 14
- **B** 11
- **C** 9
- **D** 7

12   Who is the head of the Commonwealth?

- **A** The Secretary of the Commonwealth
- **B** The Archbishop of Canterbury
- **C** The Queen
- **D** The British Prime Minister

13   What is the speed limit for cars and motorcycles in built-up areas?

- **A** 60 miles per hour
- **B** 30 miles per hour
- **C** 50 miles per hour
- **D** 70 miles per hour

14   Is the statement below TRUE or FALSE?
There are 2 million children at work in the UK at any one time.

- **A** True
- **B** False

15   Which TWO of the following are National Insurance contributions used for?

- **A** To contribute to your State Pension
- **B** To help fund the National Health Service
- **C** To pay for education and community services
- **D** To pay for police and the armed forces

16   Which of the following parliaments or assemblies use proportional representation?

- **A** European Parliament
- **B** Northern Ireland Assembly
- **C** Scottish Parliament
- **D** All of the above

17 Is the statement below
TRUE or FALSE?
*Everyone living in the UK has
the responsibility of attending
jury service when called upon.*

- **A** True
- **B** False

18 Which one of the following
parliaments or assemblies
does not use proportional
representation?

- **A** House of Commons
- **B** Scottish Parliament
- **C** Welsh Assembly
- **D** Northern Ireland Assembly

19 Is the statement below
TRUE or FALSE?
*Young people who have been
unemployed for 18 months are
usually required to join New Deal.*

- **A** True
- **B** False

20 Why did Britain admit 28,000
people of Indian origin in the
late 1960s and early 1970s?

- **A** They were escaping religious
  persecution
- **B** They were forced to leave
  Uganda
- **C** To address shortages in skilled
  labour
- **D** Because of an agreement with
  the Indian government

21 Which of these statements
is correct?

- **A** Some young people work to
  pay for their university fees
  and expenses.
- **B** University education is free to
  anyone who wishes to study.

22 Is the statement below
TRUE or FALSE?
*The use of hard drugs has a strong
link to causes of mental illness.*

- **A** True
- **B** False

23 Is the statement below
TRUE or FALSE?
*In Northern Ireland, the cost
of water supply is included
in domestic rates.*

- **A** True
- **B** False

24 Who is the Head of State
of the United Kingdom?

- **A** The Home Secretary
- **B** The Speaker of the House of
  Commons
- **C** The King or Queen
- **D** The Prime Minister

Answers: Practice Test 12

1	A	10%
2	D	18–65 years old
3	B	ESOL
	D	Numeracy
4	B	False
5	B	The birth of Jesus Christ
6	B	False
7	A	Moderator
8	C	2,500
9	B	True
10	B	False
11	A	14
12	C	The Queen
13	B	30 miles per hour
14	A	True
15	A	To contribute to your State Pension
	B	To help fund the National Health Service
16	D	All of the above
17	B	False
18	A	House of Commons
19	B	False
20	B	They were forced to leave Uganda
21	A	Some young people work to pay for their university fees and expenses.
22	A	True
23	A	True
24	C	The King or Queen

Practice Test 13

1 At what age can children in the UK choose to leave school?

- A 12
- B 18
- C 16
- D 14

2 How many Members of the Scottish Parliament (MSPs) are there?

- A 158
- B 97
- C 105
- D 129

3 Which TWO of the following policy areas have not been transferred to the Welsh Assembly or the Scottish Parliament and remain under central UK Government control?

- A Defence
- B Education
- C Foreign affairs
- D Health

4 Is the statement below TRUE or FALSE?
Citizens of an EU member state have the right to travel to and work in any EU country if they have a valid passport or identity card.

- A True
- B False

5 Is the statement below TRUE or FALSE?
It is not possible to choose between electricity and gas suppliers.

- A True
- B False

6 Which of the following is not an agreement produced by the UN?

- A Universal Declaration of Human Rights
- B UN Convention on the Rights of the Child
- C Convention for the Protection of the Ozone Layer
- D Convention on the Elimination of All Forms of Discrimination against Women

7 Which of these statements is correct?

- A Everyone in the UK has to pay for eye sight tests and glasses.
- B Eye sight tests and glasses are free to anyone over 60 years old.

8 **If you have been dismissed from your job unfairly, how long do you have to take your case to an Employment Tribunal?**

A One month

B Two months

C Three months

D Six months

9 **Which of these statements is correct?**

A Tickets for trains are usually bought before you get on the train.

B Tickets for trains are usually bought when you have reached your destination.

10 **Is the statement below TRUE or FALSE?**
In Northern Ireland, a newly qualified driver must display an R-plate for one year after passing the test.

A True

B False

11 **Is the statement below TRUE or FALSE?**
People have to buy a TV licence for each individual TV they own.

A True

B False

12 **Which TWO of the following should you do if you are involved in a road accident?**

A Admit that the accident was your fault

B Exchange your driving licence with the other drivers

C Give your details to the other drivers

D Make a note of everything that happened and contact your insurance company

13 **Is the statement below TRUE or FALSE?**
Women have had equal voting rights with men in the UK since 1928.

A True

B False

14 **What traditionally happens on April Fool's Day?**

A It is a public holiday until noon

B People play jokes on each other

C People enjoy public fireworks displays

D None of the above

15 **Which of these statements is correct?**

A Parents are allowed to withdraw their children from religious education lessons.

B Schools can choose to provide religious education to pupils.

16 Which TWO of the following constitute the UK Parliament?

- **A** The House of Commons
- **B** The Cabinet
- **C** The House of Lords
- **D** The civil service

17 Is the statement below TRUE or FALSE?
If an employee's work, punctuality or attendance does not improve, after being given a warning, then their employer can give them notice to leave their job.

- **A** True
- **B** False

18 What is the name of the system that governs how MPs are elected into the House of Commons?

- **A** Electoral college system
- **B** Proportional representation system
- **C** 'First past the post' system
- **D** Aggregated vote system

19 From which TWO of the following can you get further information about welfare benefits?

- **A** A bank
- **B** A building society
- **C** Citizens Advice Bureau
- **D** Jobcentre Plus

20 Is the statement below TRUE or FALSE?
It is not customary for job applicants to ask questions during a job interview.

- **A** True
- **B** False

21 Which of these statements is correct?

- **A** The Geordie dialect originates from Tyneside.
- **B** The Geordie dialect originates from Merseyside.

22 What percentage of Christians in the UK are Roman Catholic?

- **A** 10%
- **B** 40%
- **C** 30%
- **D** 20%

23 What is the standard closing time of a pub?

- **A** 1am
- **B** 11pm
- **C** 2am
- **D** 10pm

24 Is the statement below TRUE or FALSE?
The Leader of the Opposition is not allowed to ask questions during Prime Minister's Questions.

- **A** True
- **B** False

Answers: Practice Test 13

1	C	16
2	D	129
3	A	Defence
	C	Foreign affairs
4	A	True
5	B	False
6	C	Convention for the Protection of the Ozone Layer
7	B	Eye sight tests and glasses are free to anyone over 60 years old.
8	C	Three months
9	A	Tickets for trains are usually bought before you get on the train.
10	A	True
11	B	False
12	C	Give your details to the other drivers
	D	Make a note of everything that happened and contact your insurance company
13	A	True
14	B	People play jokes on each other
15	A	Parents are allowed to withdraw their children from religious education lessons.
16	A	The House of Commons
	C	The House of Lords
17	A	True
18	C	'First past the post' system
19	C	Citizens Advice Bureau
	D	Jobcentre Plus
20	B	False
21	A	The Geordie dialect originates from Tyneside.
22	A	10%
23	B	11pm
24	B	False

Practice Test 14

1 Is the statement below TRUE or FALSE?
The law states that every UK household must complete a census form.

 A True

B False

2 Which TWO places can you get visits from or meet with a Health Visitor?

A In your home

B At a clinic

C At a nursery school

D In your local community centre

3 Is the statement below TRUE or FALSE?
The government can tell the police how to deal with a particular case.

A True

B False

4 When is Mother's Day?

 A The Sunday four weeks before Easter

B The Saturday four weeks before Easter

C The Sunday one week before Easter

D The Sunday three weeks before Easter

5 Is the statement below TRUE or FALSE?
The Prime Minister and most members of the Cabinet are MPs.

 A False

B True

6 What is the current minimum age for standing for public office?

A 18 years

B 25 years

C 30 years

D 21 years

7 When are by-elections held?

A Every two years

B Every five years

C Only if an MP dies or resigns during their term

D Only if MPs pass a vote of no confidence in the Prime Minister

8 Is the statement below TRUE or FALSE?
Welsh is no longer taught in schools in Wales.

A False

B True

9 Is the statement below
TRUE or FALSE?
*Any child under school-leaving
age seeking to do paid work
must apply for a licence
from the local authority.*

 A   True

 B   False

10 What does the abbreviation
FA stand for?

A   The Fine Arts

B   A Federal Agent

C   The Fourth Amendment

D   The Football Association

11 Who will provide the legal
agreements necessary for
you to buy a home?

A   The local authority

B   A solicitor

C   A bank

D   A surveyor

12 Is the statement below
TRUE or FALSE?
*You need an appointment to
visit an NHS walk-in centre.*

A   True

B   False

13 Which of the following is it
compulsory to have insurance for?

A   If you have a credit card

B   If you plan to travel abroad

C   If you have a car or motorcycle

D   If you use a mobile phone

14 Is the statement below
TRUE or FALSE?
*People who buy their own
homes using a mortgage usually
pay this back within 15 years.*

 A   True

B   False

15 What is the minimum number
of weeks of maternity leave
that women are entitled to?

A   11 weeks

B   16 weeks

C   21 weeks

D   26 weeks

16 Which of the following
positions in parliament is
NOT part of the Cabinet?

A   Chancellor of the Exchequer

B   Lord Chancellor

C   Leader of the Opposition

D   Home Secretary

17 What does Guy Fawkes
Night commemorate?

A   Remembrance of those killed
during war

B   The invention of fireworks

C   The failure of a plot to bomb
parliament

D   The rebuilding of the Houses
of Parliament

18 Is the statement below TRUE or FALSE?
A tenancy agreement will be for a fixed period of time.

A True
B False

19 Which of these statements is correct?

A Your entitlement to redundancy pay depends on the length of time you have been employed.
B If you lose your job, you will always be entitled to redundancy pay.

20 In Scotland, when do most young people take SQA examinations?

A 17 years old
B 15 years old
C 16 years old
D 18 years old

21 A terrible famine occurred in Ireland during the middle of which decade?

A 1880s
B 1860s
C 1840s
D 1890s

22 What does the film classification U mean?

A No one under 18 is allowed to see or rent the film
B Suitable for everyone but some parts of the film might be unsuitable for children
C Suitable for anyone aged four years or over
D Children under 15 are not allowed to see or rent the film

23 Is the statement below TRUE or FALSE?
Over the last 20 years, there has been a decline in population in the North East and North West of England.

A False
B True

24 What type of constitution does the UK have?

A An unwritten constitution
B An amended constitution
C A written constitution
D A legal constitution

Answers: Practice Test 14

1	A	True
2	A	In your home
	B	At a clinic
3	B	False
4	D	The Sunday three weeks before Easter
5	B	True
6	A	18 years
7	C	Only if an MP dies or resigns during their term
8	A	False
9	A	True
10	D	The Football Association
11	B	A solicitor
12	B	False
13	C	If you have a car or motorcycle
14	B	False
15	D	26 weeks
16	C	Leader of the Opposition
17	C	The failure of a plot to bomb parliament
18	A	True
19	A	Your entitlement to redundancy pay depends on the length of time you have been employed.
20	C	16 years old
21	C	1840s
22	C	Suitable for anyone aged four years or over
23	B	True
24	A	An unwritten constitution

Practice Test 15

1 Which of these statements is correct?

- **A** The interest charged on store cards is usually very low.
- **B** A store card is like a credit card but used only in a specific shop.

2 Which three countries did Jewish people migrate from (and into the UK) to escape persecution during 1880–1910?

- **A** China, Japan, Korea
- **B** Israel, Egypt, Jordan
- **C** USA, Canada, Mexico
- **D** Poland, Ukraine, Belarus

3 Is the statement below TRUE or FALSE?
Guidance regarding who is allowed to work in the UK can be obtained from the Department for Work and Pensions.

- **A** True
- **B** False

4 When are elections for Members of the European Parliament (MEPs) held?

- **A** Every year
- **B** Every three years
- **C** Every four years
- **D** Every five years

5 Is the statement below TRUE or FALSE?
A jury decides whether someone is innocent or guilty of a serious crime.

- **A** True
- **B** False

6 How do you register to vote?

- **A** Bring your passport to any polling booth on election day
- **B** Contact your local MP's office
- **C** Do nothing – all eligible citizens are automatically registered
- **D** Contact your local council election registration office

7 Which of these statements is correct?

- **A** It is compulsory for children aged between 5 and 16 to receive full-time education.
- **B** Children aged over 14 do not have to receive full-time education.

8 Why did Protestant Huguenots from France come to Britain?

- **A** To invade and seize land
- **B** To escape religious persecution
- **C** To seek refuge from war
- **D** To escape famine

9　**What is the name of the official record of proceedings in parliament?**

- A　Parliament News
- B　Hansard
- C　Westminster Hour
- D　The Recorder

10　**What age do children in Scotland start secondary school?**

- A　10
- B　11
- C　12
- D　13

11　**Is the statement below TRUE or FALSE?**
In Wales, free dental treatment is available to all people.

- A　True
- B　False

12　**What age must you be to buy a lottery ticket?**

- A　16 years old
- B　17 years old
- C　18 years old
- D　21 years old

13　**Who are welfare benefits not available to?**

- A　The unemployed
- B　People who do not have legal rights of residence in the UK
- C　The elderly
- D　The sick and disabled

14　**Is the statement below TRUE or FALSE?**
The Leader of the Opposition leads the political party in power.

- A　True
- B　False

15　**Where is the Geordie dialect spoken?**

- A　Tyneside
- B　Cornwall
- C　Liverpool
- D　London

16　**Is the statement below TRUE or FALSE?**
Secondary schools are smaller than primary schools.

- A　True
- B　False

17　**Is the statement below TRUE or FALSE?**
Few young people have part-time jobs while they are still at school.

- A　True
- B　False

18　**How is the NHS Direct service provided?**

- A　Over the telephone
- B　Using a mobile surgery or ambulance
- C　At your GP's surgery
- D　At your nearest hospital

19 **Which TWO of the following organisations are pressure groups?**

(A) National Union of Teachers

(B) Conservative Party

(C) Department for Environment, Food and Rural Affairs

(D) Greenpeace

20 **What percentage of children in the UK attend independent schools?**

(A) About 8%

(B) About 22%

(C) About 40%

(D) About 95%

21 **For which TWO of the following are you likely to be required to prove your identity?**

(A) When applying for Housing Benefit

(B) When opening a bank account

(C) When purchasing National Rail tickets

(D) When travelling between England and Wales

22 **What does the film classification PG mean?**

(A) Suitable for everyone but some parts of the film might be unsuitable for children

(B) No one under 18 is allowed to see or rent the film

(C) Children under 15 are not allowed to see or rent the film

(D) Suitable for anyone aged four years or over

23 **At what voltage is electricity supplied to homes in the UK?**

(A) 50 volts

(B) 110 volts

(C) 240 volts

(D) 1,000 volts

24 **How many weeks of paid paternity leave are fathers (who have worked for their employer for at least 26 weeks) entitled to?**

(A) One week

(B) Two weeks

(C) Three weeks

(D) Four weeks

Answers: Practice Test 15

1	B	A store card is like a credit card but used only in a specific shop.
2	D	Poland, Ukraine, Belarus
3	B	False
4	D	Every five years
5	A	True
6	D	Contact your local council election registration office
7	A	It is compulsory for children aged between 5 and 16 to receive full-time education.
8	B	To escape religious persecution
9	B	Hansard
10	C	12
11	B	False
12	A	16 years old
13	B	People who do not have legal rights of residence in the UK
14	B	False
15	A	Tyneside
16	B	False
17	B	False
18	A	Over the telephone
19	A	National Union of Teachers
	D	Greenpeace
20	A	About 8%
21	A	When applying for Housing Benefit
	B	When opening a bank account
22	A	Suitable for everyone but some parts of the film might be unsuitable for children
23	C	240 volts
24	B	Two weeks

Practice Test 16

1 Is the statement below TRUE or FALSE?
All candidates standing for office in local government must be members of a political party.

- **A** True
- **B** False

2 What is the name of the patron saint of Scotland?

- **A** St Patrick
- **B** St George
- **C** St Andrew
- **D** St David

3 Which of these statements is correct?

- **A** Boxing Day and New Year's Day are both public holidays.
- **B** New Year's Day is a public holiday and Boxing Day is not.

4 Who has responsibility for making sure children go to school, arrive on time and attend school for the whole school year?

- **A** The police
- **B** The child's teacher
- **C** The child's parent or guardian
- **D** The local authority

5 When is Christmas celebrated?

- **A** 25 November
- **B** 1 January
- **C** 24 December
- **D** 25 December

6 What work did migrant Irish labourers do in the UK during the Irish famine?

- **A** Teach in schools
- **B** Drive local buses
- **C** Build canals and railways
- **D** Work in textile mills

7 In Northern Ireland, who is responsible for investigating serious complaints against the police?

- **A** The Police Ombudsman
- **B** The Lord Chancellor
- **C** The Chief of Police
- **D** The Home Secretary

8 What does NHS stand for?

- **A** National Hockey Stadium
- **B** National Health Service
- **C** New Homes Show
- **D** National Horse Show

9   **Which TWO of the following may prevent you from being able to stand for public office?**

 A   Having been found guilty of a criminal offence

 B   Being a member of the armed forces

 C   Being a Commonwealth citizen

D   Being a citizen of the Irish Republic

10   **What is the population of Northern Ireland?**

 A   0.9 million

B   2.5 million

C   3.1 million

D   1.7 million

11   **Which denomination of bank notes does not exist in the UK?**

A   £2

B   £5

C   £50

D   £20

12   **Is the statement below TRUE or FALSE?**
It is a criminal offence to drive away after an accident without stopping.

 A   True

B   False

13   **What proportion of the UK population have used illegal drugs at one time or another?**

 A   One-half

B   Two-thirds

 C   One-quarter

D   One-third

14   **Is the statement below TRUE or FALSE?**
There are more people over 60 in the UK than children under 16.

A   True

B   False

15   **Which of these statements is correct?**

A   Antenatal care is only available from special private clinics and is not part of the NHS.

B   You can get regular antenatal care from your local hospital, local health centre or from special antenatal clinics.

16   **In which year did Queen Elizabeth II start her reign?**

A   1972

B   1963

C   1952

D   1945

17 What is the purpose of the United Nations?

- **A** To create global laws to regulate foreign affairs
- **B** To create a single market for all world nations
- **C** To debate global third world development and funding proposals
- **D** To prevent war and promote international peace and security

18. How much has the UK population grown by (in percentage terms) since 1971?

- **A** 7.7%
- **B** 2.9%
- **C** 34.1%
- **D** 23.5%

19 Which of these statements is correct?

- **A** In an emergency you can attend a hospital, but only if you have a letter from your GP.
- **B** In an emergency you should go to the Accident and Emergency department of your nearest hospital.

20 Which TWO of the following pieces of information are collected during a census?

- **A** Health
- **B** Income
- **C** Political beliefs
- **D** Marital status

21 Where is the Scouse dialect spoken?

- **A** Cornwall
- **B** London
- **C** Liverpool
- **D** Tyneside

22 In what year did the Prime Minister gain powers to nominate members of the House of Lords?

- **A** 1980
- **B** 1968
- **C** 1973
- **D** 1958

23 What is the speed limit for cars and motorcycles on motorways and dual carriageways?

- **A** 70 miles per hour
- **B** 50 miles per hour
- **C** 100 miles per hour
- **D** 60 miles per hour

24 Is the statement below TRUE or FALSE?
If you buy a home with a mortgage, you must insure the building.

- **A** True
- **B** False

Answers: Practice Test 16

1	B	False
2	C	St Andrew
3	A	Boxing Day and New Year's Day are both public holidays.
4	C	The child's parent or guardian
5	D	25 December
6	C	Build canals and railways
7	A	The Police Ombudsman
8	B	National Health Service
9	A	Having been found guilty of a criminal offence
	B	Being a member of the armed forces
10	D	1.7 million
11	A	£2
12	A	True
13	D	One-third
14	A	True
15	B	You can get regular antenatal care from your local hospital, local health centre or from special antenatal clinics.
16	C	1952
17	D	To prevent war and promote international peace and security
18	A	7.7%
19	B	In an emergency you should go to the Accident and Emergency department of your nearest hospital.
20	A	Health
	D	Marital Status
21	C	Liverpool
22	D	1958
23	A	70 miles per hour
24	A	True

Practice Test 17

1 Suffragettes campaigned and demonstrated in the late 19th and early 20th centuries for which right?

- A The right to vote
- B The right to equal pay as men
- C The right to join the war effort
- D The right to work

2 Is the statement below TRUE or FALSE?
A country cannot be expelled from the Council of Europe.

- A True
- B False

3 What must you complete to gain an AS-level?

- A Three AS units
- B Two AS units
- C Three GCSEs
- D Two GCSEs

4 At which TWO of the following places can you apply for a National Insurance number?

- A Any Jobcentre Plus branch
- B Your local council or town hall
- C Your local library
- D Your local Social Security Office

5 Is the statement below TRUE or FALSE?
Ulster Scots is a dialect which is spoken in Scotland.

- A True
- B False

6 How many countries are members of the European Union?

- A 15 countries
- B 12 countries
- C 41 countries
- D 27 countries

7 Which TWO of the following are public holidays in England?

- A 1 January
- B 2 January
- C 23 April
- D 25 December

8 In which year did the NHS begin?

- A 1939
- B 1948
- C 2000
- D 1911

**9   Is the statement below
TRUE or FALSE?**
*You may only attend a further
education college if you are
less than 18 years old.*

- **A** True
- **B** False

**10 When might you need
a CRB check?**

- **A** When applying for welfare
benefits
- **B** When buying a house
- **C** When requesting medical
treatment from the NHS
- **D** When applying for work that
involves children or vulnerable
people

**11 Is the statement below
TRUE or FALSE?**
*There are more men than
women in Britain.*

- **A** True
- **B** False

**12 Which of these statements
is correct?**

- **A** Education at state schools
in the UK is free. There are
no extra charges for music
lessons, school outings or
school uniforms.
- **B** Education at state schools in
the UK is free, but parents
have to pay for school
uniforms and sports wear.

13 When is Remembrance Day?

- **A** 31 August
- **B** 21 October
- **C** 11 November
- **D** 1 May

**14 What are you called if you need
to stay overnight in hospital?**

- **A** An outpatient
- **B** A night patient
- **C** An in-patient
- **D** A day patient

**15 Which TWO of the following
statements are correct about
political reporting during
election periods in the UK?**

- **A** Television channels have
to give equal time to rival
viewpoints
- **B** Politicians must be able to
read interview questions
beforehand
- **C** It is illegal for newspapers to
run campaigns to influence
people's opinions
- **D** All reporting on radio and
television must be balanced

**16 Is the statement below
TRUE or FALSE?**
*In Northern Ireland, it is
illegal to discriminate on
grounds of religious belief
or political opinion.*

- **A** True
- **B** False

17 Is the statement below
TRUE or FALSE?
*To become a local councillor,
a candidate must have a local
connection with the area.*

A True

B False

18 To which TWO of the following
countries did textile and
engineering firms from
the UK send recruitment
agents during the 1950s?

A Poland

B Pakistan

C South Africa

D India

19 Which of these statements
is correct?

A You must be 16 or 17 years
old to be eligible for a Young
Person's Bridging Allowance.

B You must be at least 18 years
old to be eligible for a Young
Person's Bridging Allowance.

20 Is the statement below
TRUE or FALSE?
*It is illegal to drive whilst
holding a mobile phone.*

A True

B False

21 What are TWO stages that you
must complete before you can
get a full driving licence?

A Pass a breathalyser test

B Pass a practical driving test

C Pass a written theory test

D Pass an MOT test

22 What is the title of the
King or Queen within the
Church of England?

A Head Priest

B Archbishop of Canterbury

C Supreme Governor

D Governor General

23 Is the statement below
TRUE or FALSE?
*The Council of Europe has
no power to make laws.*

A True

B False

24 Is the statement below
TRUE or FALSE?
*It is not possible to see the
electoral register as this would
damage the privacy of voters.*

A True

B False

Answers: Practice Test 17

1	A	The right to vote
2	B	False
3	A	Three AS units
4	A	Any Jobcentre Plus branch
	D	Your local Social Security Office
5	B	False
6	D	27 countries
7	A	1 January
	D	25 December
8	B	1948
9	B	False
10	D	When applying for work that involves children or vulnerable people
11	B	False
12	B	Education at state schools in the UK is free, but parents have to pay for school uniforms and sports wear.
13	C	11 November
14	C	An in-patient
15	A	Television channels have to give equal time to rival viewpoints
	D	All reporting on radio and television must be balanced
16	A	True
17	A	True
18	B	Pakistan
	D	India
19	A	You must be 16 or 17 years old to be eligible for a Young Person's Bridging Allowance.
20	A	True
21	B	Pass a practical driving test
	C	Pass a written theory test
22	C	Supreme Governor
23	A	True
24	B	False

Practice Test 18

1 Which of the UK national days is celebrated with a public holiday?

 A St Patrick's Day in Northern Ireland

B St Andrew's Day in Scotland

C St George's Day in England

D St David's Day in Wales

2 From where did the government encourage immigrant workers to help British reconstruction after the Second World War?

A Australia and other parts of Oceania

B The USA and other parts of North America

C Ireland, other parts of Europe and the West Indies

D India, Pakistan and Bangladesh

3 Is the statement below TRUE or FALSE?
Applications for council housing are assessed according to individual needs. This is done through a system of points. You get more points if you have children, are homeless or have chronic ill health.

A True

B False

4 Is the statement below TRUE or FALSE?
If you do not pay your electricity bill and the supply is cut off, you can be reconnected for free.

 A True

B False

5 How many children are estimated to be working in the United Kingdom?

A 8 million

B 5 million

C 2 million

D 1 million

6 Which of the following statements is correct?

A As soon as you become self-employed you should register yourself for National Insurance and tax by contacting HM Revenue & Customs.

B It is not necessary to contact HM Revenue & Customs when you become self-employed.

7 What do people in the UK usually do on Christmas Day?

A Spend the day at home and eat a special meal

B Fast from drinking or eating

C Enjoy fireworks displays

D Dress up in frightening costumes to play trick or treat

8 What is the main aim behind the European Union today?

- **A** For member states to protect human rights in Europe
- **B** For member states to observe a single set of laws
- **C** For member states to improve efficiency
- **D** For member states to function as a single market

9 How many bank holidays are held every year in the UK?

- **A** One
- **B** Eight
- **C** Four
- **D** Six

10 In which TWO places does the European Parliament meet?

- **A** Amsterdam
- **B** Strasbourg
- **C** Berlin
- **D** Brussels

11 Is the statement below TRUE or FALSE?
The Church of England is called the Episcopal Church in Scotland.

- **A** True
- **B** False

12 When did the government start a programme of devolved administration for Wales and Scotland?

- **A** 1982
- **B** 1997
- **C** 1979
- **D** 2001

13 Is the statement below TRUE or FALSE?
All debates within the Houses of Parliament are private and cannot be attended by members of the public.

- **A** True
- **B** False

14 How many young people (up to the age of 19) are there in the UK?

- **A** 5 million
- **B** 10 million
- **C** 15 million
- **D** 20 million

15 Is the statement below TRUE or FALSE?
Parents are not allowed to get involved in a school's governing body.

- **A** True
- **B** False

16 **Which TWO of the following can you contact to find the name of a dentist?**

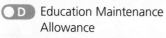

- **A** Your GP's practice
- **B** NHS Direct
- **C** Citizens Advice Bureau
- **D** Local authority

17 **Why is it important to use a solicitor when buying a property?**

- **A** They will check that the property is structurally sound
- **B** They will carry out legal checks on the property, the seller and the local area
- **C** They will arrange the mortgage with your bank
- **D** They will negotiate a better price from the estate agent

18 **What is the financial help called that is available to young people from low-income families to help them with their studies after they leave school at 16?**

- **A** Housing Benefit
- **B** School Leaver's Payment
- **C** After-School Allowance
- **D** Education Maintenance Allowance

19 **Is the statement below TRUE or FALSE?**
When you stay overnight in hospital you need to provide your own meals.

- **A** True
- **B** False

20 **What sport is played at the Wimbledon tournament?**

- **A** Rugby
- **B** Tennis
- **C** Football
- **D** Cricket

21 **What is the maximum age that your car can be before you must take it for an MOT test each year?**

- **A** One year old
- **B** Two years old
- **C** Three years old
- **D** Four years old

22 **When was the current voting age set?**

- **A** 1956
- **B** 1982
- **C** 1945
- **D** 1969

23 **Which of these statements is correct?**

- **A** Proceedings in parliament are publicly available.
- **B** Proceedings in parliament are never made public.

24 **Where does the Scottish Parliament meet?**

- **A** Holyrood
- **B** Senedd
- **C** Chequers
- **D** Stormont

Answers: Practice Test 18

1	A	St Patrick's Day in Northern Ireland
2	C	Ireland, other parts of Europe and the West Indies
3	A	True
4	B	False
5	C	2 million
6	A	As soon as you become self-employed you should register yourself for National Insurance and tax by contacting HM Revenue & Customs.
7	A	Spend the day at home and eat a special meal
8	D	For member states to function as a single market
9	C	Four
10	B	Strasbourg
	D	Brussels
11	A	True
12	B	1997
13	B	False
14	C	15 million
15	B	False
16	B	NHS Direct
	C	Citizen's Advice Bureau
17	B	They will carry out legal checks on the property, the seller and the local area
18	D	Education Maintenance Allowance
19	B	False
20	B	Tennis
21	C	Three years old
22	D	1969
23	A	Proceedings in parliament are publicly available.
24	A	Holyrood

CHAPTER 9
After Your Test

➜ IF YOUR APPLICATION for citizenship is accepted, you will receive a Citizenship Invitation by post. You will be asked to attend your citizenship ceremony, and you have 90 days to do so. This is the last step in the process and afterwards you'll officially be a British citizen.

Your Citizenship Invitation letter will contain all the information you need to book your ceremony.

Citizenship ceremonies are hosted by the Superintendent Registrar and usually local dignitaries will also attend. The ceremonies are normally attended by a number of other new citizens. You will be allowed to bring a limited number of guests to the ceremony, usually two people.

The format of the ceremony will vary depending on the venue. In most cases there will be a welcome speech. Then you will be asked to stand and swear the oath of allegiance or, if you prefer, to speak the affirmation of allegiance. You will also be asked to take the Citizenship Pledge. Some ceremonies will perform the oaths, affirmations and pledges as a group, others will go around each member of the group individually.

OATH OF ALLEGIANCE

I (name) swear by Almighty God that on becoming a British citizen, I will be faithful and bear true allegiance to Her Majesty Queen Elizabeth the Second, her Heirs and Successors, according to law.

AFFIRMATION OF ALLEGIANCE

I (name) do solemnly, sincerely and truly declare and affirm that on becoming a British citizen, I will be faithful and bear true allegiance to Her Majesty Queen Elizabeth the Second, her Heirs and Successors, according to law.

CITIZENSHIP PLEDGE

I will give my loyalty to the United Kingdom and respect its rights and freedoms. I will uphold its democratic values. I will observe its laws faithfully and fulfil my duties and obligations as a British citizen.

The national anthem will then be played and may be sung as a group – depending on the organisation of the ceremony. Either way, all British citizens should know the words. It is very short – only 29 words long.

GOD SAVE THE QUEEN

God save our gracious Queen,
Long live our noble Queen,
God save the Queen:
Send her victorious,
Happy and glorious,
Long to reign over us:
God save the Queen.

Finally, you will be presented with your citizenship certificate and an information pack. Many people like to remember this formal occasion and take photographs – this is definitely encouraged! It has taken a long time to get to this point so make sure you enjoy it.

Professional photographers may attend your ceremony and offer good-quality photographs. Alternatively, if you bring your own camera, there will be many people at the event who will be happy to take your photograph.

Applying for a British passport

Now that you are officially a British citizen, you can apply for a British passport. This is a relatively simple matter. However, the increase in passport fraud and identity theft has meant that there are more checks to process new applications.

The Identity and Passport Service (IPS) have introduced interviews for all first-time applicants for a British passport. The interview is to verify your identity by getting you to confirm details about your background and past history. Details about booking an interview will be sent to you after your application has been received by the IPS. The interview should take 30 minutes and is free of charge. The IPS recommend that you allow six weeks to obtain a passport, and not to book any travel arrangements until the new passport is received.

You can get an application form for a British passport using the following methods:

• Collect a form from selected Post Office branches

• Fill in the online application form request to receive a form in the post

• Call the IPS Passport Adviceline: 0300 222 0000

• Go online and submit your details using the online application form at www.direct.gov.uk/passports

If you fill in your form online, you get the benefit of interactive help while completing your form. It's also much easier to correct mistakes. Once you've finished submitting your details online, the form is printed and sent to you. Your application will need to be countersigned by a British citizen of good standing who has known you for at least two years. All you need to do then is attach your supporting documents and submit your application.

Before sending your application, make sure your photographs comply with new biometric regulations. There are strict guidelines for photographs and it is recommended that you visit an experienced passport photo retailer to have your photograph taken.

There are several different ways that you can submit your passport application. These have different turnaround times and fees. Full details of these fees will be included with your application form.

Look out for the 'Check and Send' service that is available at selected Post Office branches throughout the UK. This is very popular – almost half of all people making a UK Passport application use this service. Your application is checked for errors and given priority treatment by the IPS. The service costs £8.17 and includes the postage costs for your application.